PRIVATE LIVES

An Intimate Comedy in Three Acts

by

NOËL COWARD

SAMUEL   FRENCH

LONDON

NEW YORK   TORONTO   SYDNEY   HOLLYWOOD

PRIVATE LIVES

Produced at the Phoenix Theatre, London, on September 24th, 1930, with the following cast of characters:

Sibyl Chase	Adrianne Allen
Elyot Chase	Noël Coward
Victor Prynne	Laurence Olivier
Amanda Prynne	Gertrude Lawrence
Louise	Everley Gregg

The play produced by Noël Coward

This Acting Edition has been made in accordance with the production at the Apollo Theatre, London, on October 31st, 1944, in which the cast was as follows:

Sibyl Chase	Peggy Simpson
Elyot Chase	John Clements
Victor Prynne	Raymond Huntley
Amanda Prynne	Kay Hammond
Louise	Yvonne Andre

The play produced by John Clements

ACT I   The terrace of a hotel in France. A summer evening

ACT II   Amanda's flat in Paris. A few days later. Evening

ACT III The same. Next morning

ACT I

The terrace of a hotel in France

There are two french windows at the back opening on to two separate suites. The terrace space is divided by a line of small trees in tubs, and, down stage, running parallel with the footlights, there is a balustrade. Upon each side of the line of tree tubs is a set of suitable terrace furniture, two chairs, and a table. There are orange and white awnings shading the windows, as it is summer

When the CURTAIN *rises it is about 8 p.m. There is an orchestra playing not very far off. Sibyl Chase opens the windows on the* R *and steps out on to the terrace. She is very pretty and blonde, and smartly dressed in travelling clothes. She comes down stage, stretches her arms wide with a little sigh of satisfaction, puts her bag on the balustrade and regards the view with an ecstatic expression*

Sibyl (*calling*) Elli, Elli dear, do come out. It's so lovely.
Elyot (*inside*) Just a minute.

After a pause Elyot comes out. He is about thirty, quite slim and pleasant looking, and also in travelling clothes. He walks right down to the balustrade to L *of Sibyl and looks thoughtfully at the view. Sibyl slips her arm through his*

Elyot Not so bad.
Sibyl It's heavenly. Look at the lights of that yacht reflected in the water. Oh dear, I'm so happy.
Elyot (*smiling*) Are you?
Sibyl Aren't you?
Elyot Of course I am. Tremendously happy.
Sibyl Just to think, here we are, you and I, married!
Elyot Yes, things have come to a pretty pass.
Sibyl Don't laugh at me, you mustn't be *blasé* about honeymoons just because this is your second.
Elyot (*breaking* L, *frowning*) That's silly.
Sibyl Have I annoyed you by saying that?
Elyot Just a little.
Sibyl Oh, darling, I'm so sorry. (*She holds her face up to his*) Kiss me.
Elyot (*doing so and putting an arm round her shoulder*) There.
Sibyl Ummm, not so very enthusiastic.
Elyot (*kissing her again*) That better?
Sibyl Three times, please. I'm superstitious.
Elyot (*kissing her*) You really are very sweet.

Sibyl Are you glad you married me?

Elyot Of course I am.

Sibyl How glad? (*She takes a step back, holding his hand*)

Elyot Incredibly, magnificently glad.

Sibyl How lovely.

Elyot We ought to go in and dress. (*Still holding her hand he moves up stage*)

Sibyl (*moving up stage*) Gladder than before?

Elyot (*dropping her hand*) Why do you keep harping on that? (*He breaks down stage*)

Sibyl It's in my mind, and yours too, I expect.

Elyot It isn't anything of the sort. (*He sits on the chair by the tubs*)

Sybil (*coming down to the balustrade*) She was pretty, wasn't she? Amanda?

Elyot Very pretty.

Sibyl Prettier than I am?

Elyot Much.

Sibyl Elyot!

Elyot She was pretty and sleek, and her hands were long and slim, and her legs were long and slim, and she danced like an angel. You dance very poorly, by the way.

Sibyl Could she play the piano as well as I can?

Elyot She couldn't play the piano at all.

Sibyl (*triumphantly*) Aha! Had she my talent for organization?

Elyot No, but she hadn't your mother either.

Sibyl I don't believe you like Mother.

Elyot Like her! I can't bear her.

Sibyl Elyot! She's a darling, underneath.

Elyot I never got underneath.

Sibyl (*moving slightly R and running a finger along the balustrade*) It makes me unhappy to think you don't like Mother.

Elyot Nonsense. (*He rises*) I believe the only reason you married me was to get away from her.

Sibyl (*turning to him*) I married you because I loved you.

Elyot Oh dear, oh dear, oh dear, oh dear!

Sibyl (*making a slight move towards him*) I love you far more than Amanda loved you. I'd never make you miserable like she did.

Elyot (*taking out a cigarette*) We made each other miserable.

Sibyl It was all her fault, you know it was.

Elyot (*with vehemence*) Yes, it was. Entirely her fault.

Sibyl She was a fool to lose you.

Elyot We lost each other.

Sibyl She lost you, with her violent tempers and carryings on.

Elyot Will you stop talking about Amanda?

Sibyl (*moving to the chair R, and sitting*) But I'm very glad, because if she hadn't been uncontrolled, and wicked, and unfaithful, we shouldn't be here now.

Elyot She wasn't unfaithful.

Sibyl How do you know? I bet she was. I bet she was unfaithful every five minutes.

Elyot It would take a far more concentrated woman than Amanda to be unfaithful every five minutes. (*He lights a cigarette*)

Sibyl (*after a pause; anxiously*) You do hate her, don't you?

Elyot No, I don't hate her. I think I despise her.

Sibyl (*with satisfaction*) That's much worse.

Elyot (*leaning both hands on the balustrade and staring out front*) And yet I'm sorry for her.

Sibyl Why?

Elyot Because she's marked for tragedy; she's bound to make a mess of everything.

Sibyl If it's all her fault, I don't see that it matters much.

Elyot She has some very good qualities.

Sibyl Considering what a hell she made of your life, I think you are very nice about her. Most men would be vindictive.

Elyot (*moving up stage*) What's the use of that? It's all over now, such a long time ago. (*He leans against the window*)

Sibyl Five years isn't very long.

Elyot (*seriously*) Yes it is.

Sibyl (*after a pause*) Do you think you could ever love her again?

Elyot (*straightening up*) Now then, Sibyl.

Sibyl But could you?

Elyot Of course not, I love you.

Sibyl Yes, but you love me differently; I know that.

Elyot (*coming down behind her chair*) More wisely perhaps.

Sibyl I'm glad. I'd rather have that sort of love.

Elyot You're right. Love is no use unless it's wise, and kind, and un-dramatic. Something steady and sweet, to smooth out your nerves when you're tired. Something tremendously cosy—(*he sits on the table*)—and unflurried by scenes and jealousies. That's what I want, what I've always wanted really. Oh my dear, I do hope it's not going to be dull for you.

Sibyl (*putting her hand on his*) Sweetheart, as though you could ever be dull.

Elyot I'm much older than you.

Sibyl Not so very much.

Elyot Seven years.

Sibyl The music has stopped now and you can hear the sea.

Elyot We'll bathe tomorrow morning.

Sibyl (*rising and coming down to the balustrade,* L C) I mustn't get sunburnt.

Elyot Why not?

Sibyl I hate it on women.

Elyot (*rising and moving* R *round the table to the* R *end of the balustrade*) Very well, you shan't then. I hope you don't hate it on men.

Sibyl Of course I don't. It's suitable to men.

Elyot You're a completely feminine little creature, aren't you?

Sibyl Why do you say that?

Elyot Everything in its place.

Sibyl What do you mean?

Elyot If you feel you'd like me to smoke a pipe, I'll try and master it.

Sibyl I like a man to be a man, if that's what you mean.

Elyot Are you going to understand me, and manage me?

Sibyl I'm going to try to understand you.

Elyot Run me without my knowing it?

Sibyl (*withdrawing slightly*) I think you're being a little unkind.

Elyot No, I don't mean to be. I was only wondering.

Sibyl Well?

Elyot I was wondering what was going on inside your mind, what your plans are really?

Sibyl (*turning to him*) Plans; oh, Elli!

Elyot Apart from loving me and all that, you must have plans.

Sibyl I haven't the faintest idea what you're talking about.

Elyot Perhaps it's subconscious then, age-old instincts working away deep down, mincing up little bits of experience for future use, watching me carefully like a little sharp-eyed, blonde kitten.

Sibyl How can you be so horrid.

Elyot I said kitten, not cat.

Sibyl Kittens grow into cats.

Elyot Let that be a warning to you. (*He looks out front*)

Sibyl (*moving to him and slipping her arm through his again*) What's the matter, darling, are you hungry?

Elyot Not a bit.

Sibyl You're very strange all of a sudden, and rather cruel. Just because I'm feminine. It doesn't mean that I'm crafty and calculating.

Elyot I didn't say you were either of those things.

Sibyl (*breaking* L) I hate these half-masculine women who go banging about.

Elyot I hate anybody who goes banging about.

Sibyl I should think you needed a little quiet womanliness after Amanda.

Elyot (*moving away* R) Why will you keep on talking about her?

Sibyl It's natural enough, isn't it?

Elyot (*sitting on the balustrade*) What do you want to find out?

Sibyl Why did you really let her divorce you?

Elyot She divorced me for cruelty, and flagrant infidelity. I spent a whole weekend at Brighton with a lady called Vera Williams. She had the nastiest looking hair brush I have ever seen.

Sibyl Misplaced chivalry, I call it. Why didn't you divorce her?

Elyot It would not have been the action of a gentleman, whatever that may mean.

Sibyl I think she got off very lightly.

Elyot (*rising*) Once and for all will you stop talking about her.

Sibyl Yes, Elli dear.

Elyot (*facing out front*) I don't wish to see her again or hear her name mentioned.

Sibyl (*facing out front*) Very well, darling.

Elyot Is that understood?

Sibyl Yes, darling. (*She pauses*) Where did you spend your honeymoon?

Elyot St Moritz. Be quiet.

Sibyl I hate St Moritz.

Elyot So do I, bitterly.

Sibyl Was she good on skis?

Elyot (*turning to her*) Do you want to dine downstairs here, or at the Casino?

Sibyl (*crossing to him and putting her arms round his neck*) I love you, I love you, I love you.

Elyot (*completely unresponsive; moving up stage, holding her* R *hand*) Good, let's go in and dress.

Sibyl (*pulling him back*) Kiss me first.

Elyot kisses her

Elyot Casino?

Sibyl Yes. (*She collects her bag from the balustrade*) Are you a gambler? You never told me.

Elyot Every now and then.

Sibyl (*taking his arm*) I shall come and sit just behind your chair and bring you luck.

Elyot *That* will be fatal.

Sibyl exits into the suite followed by Elyot. There is a slight pause and then Victor Prynne enters from the L *suite. He is quite nice looking, about thirty or thirty-five. He is dressed in a light travelling suit. He takes three deep breaths, looks at the view, and then turns back to the window*

Victor (*calling*) Mandy!

Amanda (*inside*) What?

Victor Come outside, the view is wonderful.

Amanda I'm still damp from the bath. Wait a minute——

Victor moves to the table L *and knocks out his pipe. Presently Amanda comes out on to the terrace. She is quite exquisite with a gay face and a perfect figure. At the moment she is wearing a négligée. She comes* C

I shall catch pneumonia, that's what I shall catch.

Victor (*looking at her*) God!

Amanda I beg your pardon?

Victor You look wonderful. (*He takes her hands*)

Amanda Thank you, darling.

Victor Like a beautiful advertisement for something. (*He widens her arms*)

Amanda Nothing peculiar, I hope.

Victor I can hardly believe it's true. You and I, here alone together——

Amanda puts her head on Victor's shoulder

—married!

Amanda (*rubbing her face on his shoulder*) That stuff's very rough.

Victor Don't you like it?

Amanda A bit hearty, isn't it?

Victor Do you love me?

Amanda Of course, that's why I'm here.

Victor More than you loved ...

Amanda (*breaking* R) Now then, none of that.

Victor No, but do you love me more than you loved Elyot?

Amanda I don't remember, it's such a long time ago. (*She sits in the chair by the tubs*)

Victor Not so very long.

Amanda (*flinging out her arms*) All my life ago.

Victor I'd like to break his damned neck. (*He moves up to the windows*)

Amanda (*laughing*) Why?

Victor For making you unhappy. (*He turns to her*)

Amanda It was mutual.

Victor Rubbish! It was all his fault, you know it was.

Amanda Yes, it was, now I come to think about it.

Victor Swine! (*He comes down stage*)

Amanda Don't be so vehement, darling.

Victor I'll never treat you like that.

Amanda That's right.

Victor I love you too much.

Amanda So did he.

Victor Fine sort of love that is. He struck you once, didn't he?

Amanda More than once.

Victor Where?

Amanda Several places.

Victor (*moving slightly up stage*) What a cad.

Amanda I struck him too. Once I broke four gramophone records over his head. It was very satisfying.

Victor (*coming down stage again*) You must have been driven to distraction.

Amanda Yes, I was, but don't let's talk about it, please. After all, it's a dreary subject for our honeymoon night. (*She holds out her hand*)

Victor He didn't know when he was well off. (*He moves to her and takes her hand*)

Amanda Look at the lights of that yacht reflected in the water. I wonder whose it is.

Victor We must bathe tomorrow.

Amanda Yes. I want to get a nice sunburn.

Victor (*reproachfully*) Mandy!

Amanda Why, what's the matter?

Victor I hate sunburnt women.

Amanda Why?

Victor It's somehow, well, unsuitable.

Amanda It's awfully suitable to me, darling.

Victor Of course if you really want to. (*He moves behind her chair*)

Amanda I'm absolutely determined. I've got masses of lovely oil to rub all over myself.

Victor Your skin is so beautiful as it is. (*He kisses her neck*)

Amanda Wait and see. When I'm done a nice crisp brown, you'll fall in love with me all over again.

Victor (*moving to* C) I couldn't love you more than I do now.

Amanda Oh, dear. I did so hope our honeymoon was going to be progressive.

Victor Where did you spend the last one?

Amanda (*warningly*) Victor.

Victor I want to know.

Amanda St Moritz. It was very attractive.

Victor I hate St Moritz.

Amanda So do I.

Victor Did he start quarrelling with you right away?

Amanda Within the first few days. I put it down to the high altitudes.

Victor (*moving to her*) And you loved him?

Amanda Yes, Victor.

Victor (*putting a hand on her shoulder*) You poor child.

Amanda (*rising and crossing above the chair L*) You must try not to be pompous, dear. (*She turns away*)

Victor (*hurt*) Mandy!

Amanda I don't believe I'm a bit like what you think I am.

Victor How do you mean?

Amanda I was never a poor child.

Victor Figure of speech, dear, that's all.

Amanda I suffered a good deal, and had my heart broken. But it wasn't an innocent girlish heart. It was jagged with sophistication. I've always been sophisticated, far too knowing. That caused many of my rows with Elyot. I irritated him because he knew I could see through him.

Victor (*moving to her*) I don't mind how much you see through me.

Amanda Sweet. (*She kisses him*)

Victor (*his cheek against hers*) I'm going to make you happy.

Amanda Are you?

Victor Just by looking after you, and seeing that you're all right, you know.

Amanda (*detaching herself; a trifle wistfully*) No, I don't know.

Victor I think you love me quite differently from the way you loved Elyot.

Amanda (*coming down to the balustrade*) Do stop harping on Elyot.

Victor It's true, though, isn't it?

Amanda I love you much more calmly, if that's what you mean.

Victor More lastingly?

Amanda (*sitting on the balustrade*) I expect so. (*She holds out her L hand*)

Victor (*taking her hand and sitting on the balustrade on her R*) Do you remember when I first met you?

Amanda Yes. Distinctly.

Victor At Marion Vale's party.

Amanda Yes.

Victor Wasn't it wonderful?

Amanda Not really, dear. It was only redeemed from the completely commonplace by the fact of my having hiccoughs.

Victor I never noticed them.

Amanda Love at first sight.

Victor Where did you first meet Elyot?

Amanda (*rising and moving* L) To hell with Elyot.

Victor (*rising*) Mandy!

Amanda I forbid you to mention his name again. I'm sick of the sound of it. You must be raving mad. Here we are on the first night of our honeymoon, with the moon coming up, and the music playing, and all you can do is to talk about my first husband. It's downright sacrilegious. (*She turns away*)

Victor Don't be angry.

Amanda Well, it's very annoying.

Victor (*pulling her round*) Will you forgive me?

Amanda Yes. (*She kisses him*) Only don't do it again.

Victor I promise.

Amanda (*taking his arm*) You'd better go and dress now, you haven't bathed yet.

She leads Victor up stage

Victor Where shall we dine, downstairs here, or at the Casino?

Amanda (L *of the window*) The Casino is more fun, I think.

Victor We can play *boule* afterwards.

Amanda (*leaning against the window*) No, we can't, dear.

Victor Don't you like dear old *boule*?

Amanda No, I hate dear old *boule*. We'll play a nice game of *chemin de fer*.

Victor (R *of the window; apprehensively*) Not at the big table?

Amanda Maybe at the biggest table.

Victor You're not a terrible gambler, are you?

Amanda Inveterate. Chance rules my life.

Victor What nonsense.

Amanda How can you say it's nonsense. It was chance meeting you. It was chance falling in love; it's chance that we're here, particularly after your driving. Everything that happens is chance.

Victor You know I feel rather scared of you at close quarters.

Amanda That promises to be very embarrassing.

Victor You're somehow different now, wilder than I thought you were, more strained.

Amanda Wilder! Oh Victor, I've never felt less wild in my life. (*She crosses to the chair by the tubs*) A little strained, I grant you, but that's the newly married atmosphere; you can't expect anything else. (*She sits*) Honeymooning is a very overrated amusement.

Victor (*crossing to her*) You say that because you had a ghastly experience before.

Amanda There you go again.

Victor (*moving behind her*) It couldn't fail to embitter you a little.

Amanda The honeymoon wasn't such a ghastly experience really; it was afterwards that was so awful.

Victor (*kissing her head*) I intend to make you forget it all entirely.

Amanda You won't succeed by making constant references to it.

Victor (*breaking to* L C) I wish I knew you better.

Amanda It's just as well you don't. The "woman"—in italics—should always retain a certain amount of alluring feminine mystery for the "man"—also in italics.

Victor What about the man? Isn't he allowed to have any mystery?

Amanda Absolutely none. Transparent as glass.

Victor Oh, I see.

Amanda Never mind, darling. (*She rises and puts her arm in his*) It doesn't necessarily work out like that; it's only supposed to.

Victor I'm glad I'm normal.

Amanda What an odd thing to be glad about. Why?

Victor Well, aren't you?

Amanda I'm not so sure I'm normal.

Victor (*patting her and withdrawing his hand*) Oh, Mandy, of course you are, sweetly, divinely normal.

Amanda I haven't any peculiar cravings for Chinamen or old boots, if that's what you mean.

Victor (*scandalized*) Mandy!

Amanda (*wandering up stage*) I think very few people are completely normal really, deep down in their private lives. It all depends on a combination of circumstances. If all the various cosmic thingummys fuse at the same moment, and the right spark is struck, there's no knowing what one mightn't do. (*She comes down* R *below the chair*) That was the trouble with Elyot and me, we were like two violent acids bubbling about in a nasty little matrimonial bottle.

Victor (*following her*) I don't believe you're nearly as complex as you think you are.

Amanda I don't think I'm particularly complex, but I know I'm unreliable.

Victor You're frightening me horribly. In what way unreliable?

Amanda I'm so apt to see things the wrong way round.

Victor What sort of things?

Amanda Morals. What one should do and what one shouldn't.

Victor (*fondly*) Darling, you're so sweet. (*He kisses her cheek*)

Amanda (*patting his arm*) Thank you, Victor, that's most encouraging. (*She takes his hand*) You really must have your bath now. Come along.

Victor (*stopping*) Kiss me.

Amanda (*doing so*) There, dear, hurry now; I've only got to slip my dress on and then I shall be ready.

Victor Give me ten minutes.

Amanda I'll bring the cocktails out here when they come.

Victor All right.

Amanda Go along now, hurry.

They both disappear into their suite. After a moment's pause Elyot steps carefully on to the terrace through the window R *carrying a tray upon which are two champagne cocktails. He puts the tray down on the table*

Elyot (*calling*) Sibyl!

Sibyl (*inside*) Yes?

Elyot I've brought the cocktails out here, hurry up.

Sibyl I can't find my lipstick.

Elyot Never mind, send down to the kitchen for some cochineal.
Sibyl Don't be so silly.
Elyot Hurry up.

He saunters down to the balustrade, and looks out at the view. He looks up at the moon and sighs, then he sits down in the chair by the tubs with his back towards the line of tubs, and lights a cigarette. The orchestra is playing

> *Amanda steps gingerly on to her terrace carrying a tray with two champagne cocktails on it. She is wearing a charmingly simple evening gown. She places the tray carefully on the table. Elyot whistles. Amanda sees him, sits in her chair by the tubs and whistles too. Elyot turns; they both look at each other and rise*

Amanda Thoughtful of them to play that, wasn't it?
Elyot (*in a stifled voice*) What are you doing here?
Amanda I'm on honeymoon.
Elyot How interesting, so am I.
Amanda I hope you're enjoying it.
Elyot It hasn't started yet.
Amanda Neither has mine.
Elyot Oh, my God!
Amanda I can't help feeling that this is a little unfortunate.
Elyot Are you happy?
Amanda Perfectly. (*She clasps her hands behind her back*)
Elyot Good. That's all right, then, isn't it?
Amanda Are you?
Elyot Ecstatically. (*He clasps his hands behind his back*)
Amanda I'm delighted to hear it. We shall probably meet again sometime.
   Au revoir! (*She turns*)
Elyot (*firmly*) Good-bye.

> *Amanda exits through the window L without looking back. Elyot stands gazing after her with an expression of horror on his face. Sibyl comes brightly on to the terrace in a very pretty evening frock. She leans against the R side of the window*

Sibyl Cocktail, please.

Elyot doesn't answer

   (*As she comes down level with him*) Elli, what's the matter?

Elyot I feel very odd.
Sibyl Odd? What do you mean; ill?
Elyot Yes, ill.
Sibyl (*alarmed*) What sort of?
Elyot (*turning to her*) We must leave at once.
Sibyl Leave!
Elyot (*going to her*) Yes, dear. Leave immediately.

Sibyl Elli!

Elyot I have a strange foreboding.

Sibyl You must be mad.

Elyot (*taking her by the shoulders*) Listen, darling. I want you to be very sweet, and patient, and understanding, and not be upset, or ask any questions, or anything. I have an absolute conviction that our whole future happiness depends upon our leaving here instantly.

Sibyl Why?

Elyot I can't tell you why.

Sibyl But we've only just come.

Elyot I know that, but it can't be helped.

Sibyl What's happened, what has happened?

Elyot Nothing has happened.

Sibyl You've gone out of your mind.

Elyot I haven't gone out of my mind, but I shall if we stay here another hour.

Sibyl You're not drunk, are you?

Elyot (*breaking to the balustrade*) Of course I'm not drunk. What time have I had to get drunk?

Sibyl (*taking his hand and trying to lead him to the window*) Come down and have some dinner, darling, and then you'll feel ever so much better.

They move upstage

Elyot It's no use trying to humour me. I'm serious.

Sibyl But darling, please be reasonable. We've only just arrived; everything's unpacked. It's our first night together. We can't go away now.

Elyot We can have our first night together in Paris.

Sibyl We shouldn't get there until the small hours.

Elyot (*putting his hand on her shoulder; with a great effort at calmness*) Now please, Sibyl, I know it sounds crazy to you, and utterly lacking in reason and sense, but I've got second sight over certain things. I'm almost psychic. I've got the most extraordinary sensation of impending disaster. If we stay here something appalling will happen. I know it.

Sibyl (*crossing down stage below the chair* R; *firmly*) Hysterical nonsense.

Elyot (*crossing up stage to* L *of the window*) It isn't hysterical nonsense. Presentiments are far from being nonsense. Look at the woman who cancelled her passage on the *Titanic*. All because of a presentiment.

Sibyl I don't see what that has to do with it.

Elyot It has everything to do with it. (*He comes down stage a step or two*) She obeyed her instincts, that's what she did, and saved her life. All I ask is to be allowed to obey my instincts.

Sibyl (*facing out front*) Do you mean that there's going to be an earthquake or something?

Elyot Very possibly, very possibly indeed, or perhaps a violent explosion. (*He looks at the window* L)

Sibyl They don't have earthquakes in France.

Elyot (*coming down to the balustrade and facing out front*) On the contrary, only last week they felt a distinct shock at Antibes.

Sibyl Yes, but that's in the South where it's hot.

Elyot Don't quibble, Sibyl.

Sibyl And as for explosions, there's nothing here that can explode.

Elyot Oho, isn't there. (*He looks at the window* L)

Sibyl Yes, but Elli . . . (*She moves to him*)

Elyot (*turning and putting his hands on her shoulders*) Darling, be sweet. Bear with me. I beseech you to bear with me.

Sibyl I don't understand. It's horrid of you to do this.

Elyot I'm not doing anything. I'm only asking you, imploring you to come away from this place.

Sibyl But I love it here.

Elyot There are thousands of other places far nicer.

Sibyl (*breaking* R) It's a pity we didn't go to one of them.

Elyot Now, listen, Sibyl——

Sibyl (*moving to him*) Yes, but why are you behaving like this, why, why, why?

Elyot Don't ask why. Just give in to me. I swear I'll never ask you to give into me over anything again.

Sibyl (*with complete decision; sitting in the chair* R) I won't think of going tonight. It's utterly ridiculous. I've done quite enough travelling for one day, and I'm tired.

Elyot You're as obstinate as a mule.

Sibyl I like that, I must say.

Elyot (*hotly*) You've got your nasty little feet dug into the ground, and you don't intend to budge an inch, do you?

Sibyl (*with spirit*) No, I do not. (*She turns to him*)

Elyot If there's one thing in the world that infuriates me, it's sheer wanton stubbornness. I should like to cut off your head with a meat axe.

Sibyl (*rising*) How dare you talk to me like that, on our honeymoon night!

Elyot (*moving up stage to the window*) Damn our honeymoon night! Damn it, damn it, damn it!

Sibyl (*moving up to him; bursting into tears*) Oh, Elli, Elli——

Elyot Stop crying. Will you or will you not come away with me to Paris?

Sibyl (*coming down to the balustrade*) I've never been so miserable in my life. You're hateful and beastly. Mother was perfectly right. She said you had shifty eyes.

Elyot (*coming down to her* L) Well, she can't talk. Hers are so close together, you couldn't put a needle between them.

Sibyl (*facing him*) You don't love me a little bit. I wish I were dead.

Elyot (*facing her*) Will you or will you not come to Paris?

Sibyl No, no I won't.

Elyot Oh, my God!

He stamps indoors

Sibyl (*following him; wailing*) Oh, Elli, Elli, Elli . . .

She goes in. Victor comes stamping out of the french windows L, *followed by Amanda*

Victor (*coming down to the balustrade* R C) You were certainly right when you said you weren't normal. You're behaving like a lunatic. (*He goes up stage*)

Amanda (*following him*) Not at all. All I have done is to ask you a little favour.

Victor Little favour indeed. (*He comes down stage*)

Amanda (*moving to his* L) If we left now we could be in Paris in a few hours.

Victor If we crossed Siberia by train we could be in China in a fortnight, but I don't see any reason to do it. (*He goes up stage*)

Amanda (*following him*) Oh, Victor darling—please, please—be sensible, just for my sake.

Victor Sensible! (*He halts up* R)

Amanda (*moving to his* L) Yes, sensible. I shall be absolutely miserable if we stay here. You don't want me to be absolutely miserable all through my honeymoon, do you?

Victor But why on earth didn't you think of your sister's tragedy before?

Amanda (*coming down to the balustrade,* L *end*) I forgot.

Victor You couldn't forget a thing like that.

Amanda I got the places muddled. Then when I saw the Casino there in the moonlight—(*she points out front*)—it all came back to me.

Victor When did all this happen?

Amanda Years ago, but it might just as well have been yesterday. I can see her now lying dead, with that dreadful expression on her face. Then all that awful business of taking the body home to England. It was perfectly horrible.

Victor I never knew you had a sister.

Amanda I haven't any more.

Victor There's something behind all this.

Amanda Don't be silly. What could there be behind it.

Victor (*coming down a step*) Well, for one thing, I know you're lying.

Amanda (*turning*) Victor!

Victor Be honest. Aren't you?

Amanda (*moving away* L) I can't think how you can be so mean and suspicious.

Victor (*coming down two steps; patiently*) You're lying, Amanda. Aren't you?

Amanda (*after a quick look at him*) Yes, Victor.

Victor You never had a sister, dead or alive?

Amanda I believe there was a stillborn one in 1912.

Victor What is your reason for all this?

Amanda (*facing him*) I told you I was unreliable.

Victor Why do you want to leave so badly? (*He is now* C)

Amanda (*moving to his* L) You'll be angry if I tell you the truth.

Victor What is it?

Amanda I warn you.

Victor Tell me. Please tell me.

Amanda Elyot's here.

Victor What!

Amanda I saw him.

Victor When?

Amanda Just now, when you were in the bath.

Victor Where was he?

Amanda (*hesitatingly*) Down there, in a white suit. (*She points over the balustrade*)

Victor (*sceptically*) White suit?

Amanda (*moving away above the chair* L) Why not? It's summer, isn't it?

Victor You're lying again.

Amanda (*turning*) I'm not. He's here. (*She moves to his* L) I swear he is.

Victor Well, what of it?

Amanda I can't enjoy a honeymoon with you, with Elyot liable to bounce in at any moment.

Victor Really, Mandy.

Amanda Can't you see how awful it is? It's the most embarrassing thing that ever happened to me in my whole life.

Victor Did he see you?

Amanda No, he was running.

Victor What was he running for?

Amanda (*coming down to the balustrade* L C) How on earth do I know. Don't be so annoying.

Victor (*coming down above her*) Well, as long as he didn't see you it's all right, isn't it?

Amanda (*turning to him*) It isn't all right at all. We must leave immediately.

Victor But why?

Amanda (*crossing* R) How can you be so appallingly obstinate.

Victor I'm not afraid of him.

Amanda Neither am I. It isn't a question of being afraid. It's just a horrible awkward situation.

Victor (*coming down* L C) I'm damned if I can see why our whole honeymoon should be upset by Elyot.

Amanda My last one was.

Victor (*after a pause*) I don't believe he's here at all.

Amanda (*moving to his* R) He is, I tell you. I saw him.

Victor It was probably an optical illusion. This half light is very deceptive.

Amanda It was no such thing. (*She moves up* R, *then down* R *and up* R *again*)

Victor (*facing out front*) I absolutely refuse to change all our plans at the last moment, just because you think you've seen Elyot. It's unreasonable and ridiculous of you to demand it. Even if he is here I can't see that it matters. He'll probably feel much more embarrassed than you, and a damned good job too, and if he annoys you in any way I'll knock him down.

Amanda (*stopping up* R C) That would be charming.

Victor (*going to her*) Now don't let's talk about it any more.

Amanda Do you mean to stand there seriously and imagine that the whole thing can be glossed over as easily as that?

Victor I'm not going to leave, Mandy. If I start giving into you as early as this, our lives will be unbearable.

Amanda (*outraged*) Victor!

Victor (*calmly*) You've worked yourself up into a state over a situation which really only exists in your mind.

Amanda (*controlling herself with an effort*) Please, Victor, please, for this last time I implore you. Let's go to Paris now, tonight. I mean it with all my heart—please——

Victor (*with gentle firmness*) No, Mandy!

Amanda (*coming down* R) I see quite clearly that I have been foolish enough to marry a fat old gentleman in a club armchair.

Victor It's no use being cross.

Amanda (*crossing* L) You're a pompous ass!

Victor (*horrified*) Mandy!

Amanda (*turning on him; enraged*) Pompous ass, that's what I said, and that's what I meant. Blown out with your own importance. (*She turns away*)

Victor (*crossing to her*) Mandy, control yourself.

Amanda (*crossing* R) Get away from me. I can't bear to think I'm married to such rugged grandeur.

Victor (*after a pause; with great dignity*) I shall be in the bar. When you are ready to come down and dine, let me know.

Amanda (*turning back to the audience and leaning against the balustrade*) Go away, go away, go away.

Victor stalks off through the window L, *at the same moment that Elyot stamps on, on the other side, followed by Sibyl in tears. Elyot stands* L *of the window with his back to Amanda. Sibyl stands* R *of the window and a little inside it so that she is hidden from Amanda by Elyot*)

Elyot If you don't stop screaming, I'll murder you.

Sibyl I wish to heaven I'd never seen you in my life, let alone married you. I don't wonder Amanda left you, if you behaved to her as you've behaved to me. I'm going down to have dinner by myself and you can just do what you like about it.

Elyot Do, and I hope it chokes you.

Sibyl Oh, Elli, Elli . . .

She goes wailing indoors. Elyot stamps down to the balustrade and takes out a cigarette, obviously trying to control his nerves. Amanda sees him

Amanda Give me one, for God's sake.

Elyot gives her his cigarette and takes another for himself

Elyot Here. (*He lights her cigarette, then his own*)

Amanda I'm in such a rage.

Elyot So am I.

Amanda (*taking a puff*) What are we to do?

Elyot (*taking a puff*) I don't know.

Pause. They both puff together

Amanda Whose yacht is that?

Elyot The Duke of Westminster's I expect. It always is.

Amanda I wish I were on it.

Elyot I wish you were too.

Amanda There's no need to be nasty.

Elyot Yes there is, every need. I've never in my life felt a greater urge to be nasty.

Amanda And you've had some urges in your time, haven't you?

Elyot (*turning to her*) If you start bickering with me, Amanda, I swear I'll throw you over the edge.

Amanda (*turning to him*) Try it, that's all, just try it.

Elyot You've upset everything, as usual. (*He moves away up* R)

Amanda I've upset everything! What about you?

Elyot Ever since the first moment I was unlucky enough to set eyes on you, my life has been insupportable. (*He comes down stage*)

Amanda (*moving away up* L) Oh do shut up, there's no sense in going on like that.

Elyot Nothing's any use. There's no escape, ever. (*He moves to the table* R)

Amanda Don't be melodramatic.

Elyot Do you want a cocktail? There are two here.

Amanda There are two over here as well.

Elyot We'll have my two first.

Amanda crosses up stage into Elyot's part of the terrace. He gives her one, and keeps one himself

Amanda Shall we get roaring, screaming drunk?

Elyot I don't think that would help, we did it once before and it was a dismal failure.

Amanda It was lovely at the beginning.

Elyot You have an immoral memory, Amanda. Here's to you.

They raise their glasses solemnly and drink

Amanda I tried to get away the moment after I'd seen you, but he wouldn't budge.

Elyot What's his name?

Amanda Victor, Victor Prynne.

Elyot (*toasting*) Mr and Mrs Victor Prynne. (*He drinks*) Mine wouldn't budge either.

Amanda What's her name?

Elyot Sibyl.

Amanda (*toasting*) Mr and Mrs Elyot Chase. (*She drinks*) God pity the poor girl.

Elyot Are you in love with him?

Amanda Of course.

Elyot How funny.

Amanda I don't see anything particularly funny about it, you're in love with yours, aren't you?

Elyot Certainly.

Amanda There you are then.

Elyot (*with a look at her*) There we both are then.

A pause. Amanda crosses down R

Amanda What's she like?

Elyot Fair, very pretty, plays the piano beautifully.

Amanda Very comforting.

Elyot How's yours?

Amanda I don't want to discuss him.

Elyot Well, it doesn't matter, he'll probably come popping out in a minute and I shall see for myself. Does he know I'm here? (*He comes down to the balustrade*)

Amanda Yes, I told him.

Elyot (*with sarcasm*) That's going to make things a whole lot easier.

Amanda You needn't be frightened, he won't hurt you.

Elyot If he comes near me I'll scream the place down.

Amanda Does Sibyl know I'm here?

Elyot No, I pretended I'd had a presentiment. I tried terribly hard to persuade her to leave for Paris.

Amanda I tried too, it's lucky we didn't both succeed, isn't it? Otherwise we should probably all have joined up on the road somewhere.

Elyot (*laughing*) In some frowsy little hotel.

Amanda (*laughing too*) Oh dear, it would have been much, much worse.

Elyot (*moving to her*) I can see us all sailing down in the morning for an early start.

They both laugh intimately, moving nearer to each other. Suddenly they become aware of what is happening and stop laughing

Amanda (*after a pause*) What's happened to yours?

Elyot Didn't you hear her screaming? She's downstairs in the dining-room I think.

Amanda Mine is being grand, in the bar.

Elyot It really is awfully difficult.

A pause. Amanda sits on the balustrade

Amanda Have you known her long?

Elyot About four months, we met in a house-party in Norfolk.

Amanda Very flat, Norfolk. (*She sips her drink*)

Elyot How old is dear Victor?

Amanda Thirty-four, or five; and Sibyl?

Elyot I blush to tell you, only twenty-three.

Amanda You've gone a mucker all right.

Elyot I shall reserve my opinion of your choice until I've met dear Victor.

Amanda (*rising*) I wish you wouldn't go on calling him "Dear Victor". It's extremely irritating.

Elyot That's how I see him. Dumpy, and fair, and very considerate, with glasses. Dear Victor.

Amanda As I said before I would rather not discuss him. At least I have good taste enough to refrain from making cheap gibes at Sibyl.

Elyot You said Norfolk was flat.

Amanda That was no reflection on her, unless she made it flatter.

Elyot Your voice takes on an acid quality whenever you mention her name.

Amanda I'll never mention it again.

Elyot Good, and I'll keep off Victor.

Amanda (*with dignity*) Thank you.

There is silence for a moment. The orchestra is playing the same tune that they were playing previously

Elyot That orchestra has a remarkably small repertoire.

Amanda (*turning to him*) They don't seem to know anything but this, do they?

Elyot No.

Amanda Strange how potent cheap music is.

Elyot I'm awfully sorry about all this, really I am. I wouldn't have had it happen for the world.

Amanda I know. I'm sorry too. It's just rotten luck.

Elyot (*moving up to the window, his back to her*) I'll go away tomorrow whatever happens, so don't you worry.

Amanda That's nice of you. (*She puts down her glass and puts out her cigarette on the table* R)

Elyot I hope everything turns out splendidly for you, and that you'll be very happy.

Amanda Thank you very much. I hope the same for you, too. (*She crosses to her own side of the terrace, to* R *of her window*

There is a pause. Elyot comes down to the table R, *puts down his glass and stamps out his cigarette*

Elyot Nasty, insistent little tune.

Amanda Yes, isn't it. (*She turns and looks at him*)

Elyot (*crossing to* L *of his own window*) What exactly were you remembering at that moment?

Amanda The Palace Hotel Skating Rink in the morning, and everybody whirling round in vivid colours, and you kneeling down to put on my skates for me.

Elyot You'd fallen on your fanny a minute before.

Amanda It was beastly of you to laugh like that, I felt so humiliated.

Elyot Poor darling.

Amanda Do you remember waking up in the morning, and standing on the balcony, looking out across the valley?

A pause

Elyot Blue shadows on white snow, cleanness beyond belief, high above everything in the world. How beautiful it was.

Amanda It's nice to think we had a few marvellous moments.

Elyot A few! We had heaps really, only they slip away into the background, and one only remembers the bad ones.

Amanda Yes. What fools we were to ruin it all. What utter, utter fools.

Elyot You feel like that too, do you?

Amanda (*wearily*) Of course.

Elyot Why did we?

Amanda (*turning away*) The whole business was too much for us.

Elyot We were so ridiculously over in love.

Amanda (*turning back*) Funny, wasn't it?

Elyot (*sadly*) Horribly funny.

Amanda Selfishness, cruelty, hatred, possessiveness, petty jealousy. All those qualities came out in us just because we loved each other.

Elyot Perhaps they were there anyhow.

Amanda No, it's love that does it. To hell with love. (*She turns away*)

Elyot To hell with love. (*He turns away*)

Amanda And yet here we are starting afresh with two quite different people. In love all over again, aren't we?

Elyot doesn't answer

Aren't we? (*She turns to him*)

Elyot (*turning*) No.

Amanda Elyot.

Elyot We're not in love all over again, and you know it. Good night, Amanda. (*He turns abruptly and goes towards his own window*)

Amanda Elyot—don't be silly—come back. (*She moves above the chair by the tubs on his side of the terrace*)

Elyot (*halting*) I must go and find Sibyl.

Amanda I must go and find Victor.

Elyot (*turning to her; savagely*) Well, why don't you?

Amanda I don't want to.

Elyot It's shameful, shameful of us.

Amanda (*taking a step towards him*) Don't; I feel terrible. Don't leave me for a minute, I shall go mad if you do. (*She comes down to the balustrade L C*) We won't talk about ourselves any more, we'll talk about outside things, anything you like, only just don't leave me until I've pulled myself together.

Elyot Very well. (*He comes down to her R*)

There is dead silence for a moment

Amanda (*not looking at him*) What have you been doing lately? During these last years?

Elyot (*not looking at her*) Travelling about. I went round the world you know after——

Amanda (*hurriedly*) Yes, yes, I know. How was it?

Elyot The world?

Amanda Yes.

Elyot Oh, highly enjoyable.

Amanda China must be very interesting.

Elyot Very big, China.

Amanda And Japan——

Elyot Very small.

Amanda Did you eat sharks' fins, and take your shoes off, and use chopsticks and everything?

Elyot Practically everything. (*He turns to her*)

Amanda And India, the burning Ghars, or Ghats, or whatever they are, and the Taj Mahal. How was the Taj Mahal?

Elyot (*looking at her*) Unbelievable, a sort of dream.

Amanda (*facing him*) That was the moonlight I expect, you must have seen it in the moonlight.

Elyot (*never taking his eyes off her face*) Yes, moonlight is cruelly deceptive.

Amanda And it didn't look like a biscuit box, did it? I've always felt that it might.

Elyot (*quietly*) Darling, darling, I love you so.

Amanda And I do hope you met a sacred Elephant. They're lint white, I believe, and very, very sweet

Elyot I've never loved anyone else for an instant.

Amanda (*raising her hand feebly in protest*) No, no, you mustn't—Elyot—stop.

Elyot You love me, too, don't you? (*He moves to her*) There's no doubt about it anywhere, is there?

Amanda No, no doubt anywhere.

Elyot You're looking very lovely you know, in this damned moonlight, Amanda. Your skin is clear and cool, and your eyes are shining, and you're growing lovelier and lovelier every second as I look at you. You don't hold any mystery for me, darling, do you mind? There isn't a particle of you that I don't know, remember, and want.

Amanda (*softly*) I'm glad, my sweet.

Elyot More than any desire anywhere, deep down in my deepest heart I want you back again—please——

Amanda Don't say any more, you're making me cry so dreadfully.

Elyot pulls her gently into his arms and they stand silently, completely oblivious to everything but the moment, and each other. Then finally they separate

What now? Oh darling, what now?

Elyot I don't know, I'm lost, utterly. (*He takes a step back*)

Amanda We must think quickly, oh quickly——

Elyot Escape?

Amanda Together?

Elyot Yes, of course.

Amanda (*breaking L*) We can't, we can't, you know we can't.

Elyot (*following her*) We must.

Amanda It would break Victor's heart.

Elyot And Sibyl's too probably, that can't be helped. Think of the hell we'd lead them into if we stayed here, pretending to love them, and loving each other, so desperately.

Amanda moves above the chair by the tubs as though to cross to her own side of the terrace

Amanda We must tell them.

Elyot What?

Amanda Call them and tell them.

Elyot We can't—we can't—you know we can't. It's impossible.

Amanda It's honest.

Elyot (*moving to his own window*) I can't help how honest it is, it's too horrible to think of. How should we start? What should we say?

Amanda We should have to trust to the inspiration of the moment.

Elyot (*facing her*) It would be a moment completely devoid of inspiration. The most appalling moment imaginable.

Amanda What do you propose to do then? As it is they might appear at any moment.

Elyot We've got to decide instantly one way or another. Go away together now, or stay with them, and never see one another again, ever.

Amanda Don't be silly, what choice is there?

Elyot No choice at all, come—— (*He takes her hand and pulls her towards his window*)

Amanda No, wait. This is sheer raving madness, something's happened to us, we're not sane.

Elyot We never were.

Amanda Where can we go?

Elyot Paris first, my car's in the garage, all ready.

Amanda They'll follow us.

Elyot That doesn't matter, once the thing's done.

Amanda I've got a flat in Paris.

Elyot Good.

Amanda It's in the Avenue Montaigne. I let it to Freda Lawson, but she's in Biarritz, so it's empty.

Elyot Does Victor know?

Amanda No, he knows I have one but he hasn't the faintest idea where.

Elyot Better and better.

Amanda (*coming down to the balustrade* L C) We're being so bad, so terribly bad, we'll suffer for this, I know we shall.

Elyot Can't be helped.

Amanda Starting all those awful rows all over again.

Elyot No, no, we're older and wiser now.

Amanda What difference does that make? The first moment either of us gets a bit nervy, off we'll go again.

Elyot Stop shilly-shallying, Amanda.

Amanda I'm trying to be sensible.

Elyot You're only succeeding in being completely idiotic.

Amanda Idiotic indeed! What about you?

Elyot Now look here, Amanda——

Amanda (*stepping back; stricken*) Oh my God!

Elyot (*rushing to her*) Darling, darling, I didn't mean it . . .

Amanda (*slowly, sitting on the chair by the tubs*) I won't move from here unless we have a compact, a sacred, sacred compact never to quarrel again.

Elyot (*by the balustrade*) Easy to make but difficult to keep.

Amanda No, no, it's the bickering that always starts it. The moment we notice we're bickering, either of us, we must promise on our honour to stop dead. We'll invent some phrase or catchword, which when either of us says it, automatically cuts off all conversation for at least five minutes.

Elyot Two minutes, dear, with an option of renewal.

Amanda Very well, what shall it be?

Elyot (*hurriedly*) Solomon Isaacs.

Amanda All right, that'll do.

Elyot (*pulling her up*) Come on, come on.

They move up to the window

Amanda What shall we do if we meet either of them on the way downstairs?

Elyot Run like stags.

Amanda (*by the window*) What about clothes?

Elyot I've got a couple of bags I haven't unpacked yet.

Amanda I've got a small trunk.

Elyot Send the porter up for it.

Amanda Oh this is terrible—terrible——

Elyot Come on, come on, don't waste time.

Amanda Oughtn't we to leave notes or something?

Elyot No, no, no, we'll telegraph from somewhere on the road.

Amanda (*coming down stage*) Darling, I daren't, it's too wicked of us, I simply daren't!

Elyot (*following her down, seizing her in his arms and kissing her violently*) Now will you behave?

Amanda Yes, but Elyot darling——

Elyot Solomon Isaacs!

Elyot takes her by the hand and pulls her off through his window. After a pause Victor's voice can be heard calling, "Mandy! Mandy! Mandy!" He appears at the window L and stands nonplussed. On Victor's second "Mandy", Sibyl starts calling, "Elli! Elli! Elli!" She appears at the window R. They both stand in the C of their respective windows

Victor Good evening.

Sibyl (*rather flustered*) Good evening—I was—er—looking for my husband.

Victor Really, that's funny. I was looking for my wife.

Sibyl Quite a coincidence. (*She laughs nervously*)

Victor It's very nice here, isn't it?

Sibyl Lovely.

Victor Have you been here long?

Sibyl No, we only arrived today.

Victor Another coincidence. So did we.

Sibyl How awfully funny.

Victor (*moving to his own table*) Would you care for a cocktail?

Sibyl (*moving to her table*) Oh no thank you—really——

Victor There are two here on the table.

Sibyl glances at the two empty glasses on the balustrade, and tosses her head defiantly

Sibyl Thanks very much, I'd love one.
Victor (*crossing up* R) Good, here you are. (*He remains on his own side*)
Sibyl (*crossing up* L *and taking the cocktail*) Thank you. (*She remains on her side*)
Victor (*with rather forced gaiety*) To absent friends. (*He raises his glass*)
Sibyl (*raising hers*) To absent friends. It's awfully pretty, isn't it? The moonlight, and the lights of that yacht reflected in the water . . .
Victor I wonder who it belongs to.

the CURTAIN slowly falls

ACT II

Amanda's flat in Paris. A few days later. About ten o'clock in the evening

The flat is charmingly furnished. The principal features being a grand piano up R C, *and a large, comfortable settee down* C, *with a table and two chairs behind it. In the corner up* L, *under a china cabinet, stands another smaller settee. There is a radiogram down* L. *The window is in the corner up* R. *Down* R *is a door leading to Elyot's room. Down* L *is a door leading to Amanda's room. Double doors up* C *lead out into the hall. There is a small tub chair* L C

When the CURTAIN *rises Amanda,* R, *and Elyot,* L, *are seated opposite one another at the table. They have finished dinner and are dallying over coffee and liqueurs. Amanda wears pyjamas, and Elyot a comfortable dressing-gown*

Amanda I'm glad we let Louise go. I am afraid she is going to have a cold.

Elyot Going to have a cold; she's been grunting and snorting all the evening like a whole herd of bison.

Amanda (*thoughtfully*) Bison never sound right to me somehow. I have a feeling it ought to be bisons, a flock of bisons.

Elyot You might say a covey of bisons, or even a school of bisons.

Amanda Yes, lovely. The Royal London School of Bisons. Do you think Louise is happy at home?

Elyot No, profoundly miserable.

Amanda Family beastly to her?

Elyot (*with conviction*) Absolutely vile. Knock her about dreadfully I expect, make her eat the most disgusting food, and pull her fringe.

Amanda (*laughing*) Oh, poor Louise.

Elyot Well, you know what the French are.

Amanda Oh yes, indeed. I know what the Hungarians are, too.

Elyot What are they?

Amanda Very wistful. It's all those Pretzles, I shouldn't wonder. Have you ever crossed the Sahara on a camel?

Elyot Frequently. When I was a boy we used to do it all the time. My grandmother had a lovely seat on a camel.

Amanda There's no doubt about it, foreign travel's the thing.

Elyot (*rising and picking up the brandy bottle from the trolley*) Would you like some brandy?

Amanda Just a little.

Elyot takes out the cork, gives Amanda a slight look, pours some brandy into her glass, then some into his own

Elyot I'm glad we didn't go out tonight. (*He sits, putting the bottle on the table*)

Amanda Or last night.

Elyot Or the night before.

Amanda There's no reason to, really, when we're cosy here.

Elyot Exactly.

Amanda It's nice, isn't it?

Elyot Strangely peaceful. It's an awfully bad reflection on our characters. We ought to be absolutely tortured with conscience.

Amanda We are, every now and then.

Elyot Not nearly enough.

Amanda We sent Victor and Sibyl a nice note from wherever it was, what more can they want?

Elyot You're even more ruthless than I am.

Amanda I don't believe in crying over my bridge before I've eaten it.

Elyot Very sensible. (*He drinks*)

Amanda Personally I feel grateful for a miraculous escape. I know now that I should never have been happy with Victor. I was a fool ever to consider it.

Elyot You did a little more than consider it.

Amanda Well, you can't talk.

Elyot I wonder whether they met each other, or whether they've been suffering alone.

Amanda Oh dear, don't let's go on about it, it really does make one feel rather awful.

Elyot I suppose one or other or both of them will turn up here eventually.

Amanda Bound to; it won't be very nice, will it?

Elyot (*cheerfully*) Perfectly horrible.

Amanda (*delighted, like a child*) Do you realize that we're living in sin?

Elyot Not according to the Catholics, Catholics don't recognize divorce.

Amanda Yes, dear, but we're not Catholics.

Elyot Never mind, it's nice to think they'd sort of back us up. We were married in the eyes of Heaven, and we still are.

Amanda We may be all right in the eyes of Heaven, but we look like being in the hell of a mess socially.

Elyot Who cares?

Amanda Are we going to marry again, after Victor and Sibyl divorce us?

Elyot I suppose so. What do you think?

Amanda I feel rather scared of marriage really.

Elyot It is a frowsy business.

Amanda I believe it was just the fact of our being married, and clamped together publicly, that wrecked us before.

Elyot That, and not knowing how to manage each other.

Amanda Do you think we know how to manage each other now?

Elyot This week's been very successful. We've hardly used Solomon Isaacs at all.

Amanda Solomon Isaacs is so long, let's shorten it to Sollocks.

Elyot All right.

Amanda Darling, you do look awfully sweet in your little dressing-gown.

Elyot Yes, it's pretty ravishing, isn't it?

Amanda Do you mind if I come round and kiss you?

Elyot A pleasure, Lady Agatha.

Amanda rises, crosses to Elyot and kisses him. She stands behind his chair with her R hand on his shoulder and his L hand in hers

Amanda What fools we were to subject ourselves to five years' unnecessary suffering.

Elyot Perhaps it wasn't unnecessary, perhaps it mellowed and perfected us like beautiful ripe fruit. (*He kisses her L hand*)

Amanda (*crossing to R of the table*) When we were together, did you really think I was unfaithful to you?

Elyot Yes, practically every day.

Amanda I thought you were, too; often I used to torture myself with visions of your bouncing about on divans with awful widows. (*She stands behind her chair*)

Elyot Why widows?

Amanda I was thinking of Claire Lavenham really.

Elyot Oh Claire.

Amanda (*pushing her chair into the table; sharply*) What did you say "Oh Claire" like that for? It sounded far too careless to me.

Elyot (*wistfully*) What a lovely creature she was.

Amanda (*sitting on the R arm of the settee*) Lovely, lovely, lovely!

Elyot (*blowing her a kiss*) Darling!

Amanda Did you ever have an affair with her? Afterwards I mean?

Elyot Why do you want to know?

Amanda Curiosity, I suppose.

Elyot Dangerous.

Amanda Oh not now, not dangerous now. I wouldn't expect you to have been celibate during those five years, any more than I was.

Elyot (*stopping his glass half-way to his mouth; jumping*) What?

Amanda After all, Claire was undeniably attractive. A trifle over vivacious I always thought, but that was probably because she was fundamentally stupid.

Elyot What do you mean about not being celibate during those five years?

Amanda What do you think I mean?

Elyot (*rising*) Oh God! (*He looks down miserably*)

Amanda What's the matter?

Elyot (*moving up to the double doors*) You know perfectly well what's the matter.

Amanda (*gently*) You mustn't be unreasonable, I was only trying to stamp out the memory of you. I expect your affairs well out-numbered mine anyhow.

Elyot That is a little different. I'm a man. (*He crosses to the door down L*)

Amanda Excuse me a moment while I get a caraway biscuit and change my crinoline.

Elyot It doesn't suit women to be promiscuous.

Amanda It doesn't suit men for women to be promiscuous.

Elyot (*with sarcasm*) Very modern, dear; really your advanced views quite
    startle me. (*He moves up* L)
Amanda (*playing with the edge of a cushion, trying not to have a row*)
    Don't be cross, Elyot, I haven't been so dreadfully loose actually. Five
    years is a long time, and even if I did nip off with someone every now
    and again, they were none of them very serious.
Elyot (*coming down* L) Oh, do stop it please——
Amanda (*rising*) Well, what about you?
Elyot Do you want me to tell you?
Amanda No, no, I don't—I take everything back—I don't.
Elyot (*moving in front of the settee,* L *end; viciously*) I was madly in love
    with a woman in South Africa.
Amanda (*moving in front of the settee,* R *end*) Did she have a ring through
    her nose?
Elyot Don't be revolting.
Amanda We're tormenting one another. Sit down, sweet, I'm scared.
Elyot (*slowly*) Very well. (*He sits down slowly at the* L *end of the settee*)

Amanda sits at the R *end of the settee*

Amanda We should have said Sollocks ages ago.
Elyot We're in love all right.
Amanda Don't say it so bitterly. Let's try to get the best out of it this time,
    instead of the worst.
Elyot (*stretching his hand across*) Hand please.
Amanda (*clasping it*) Here.
Elyot (*leaning back*) More comfortable.
Amanda (*leaning back*) Much more.
Elyot (*after a slight pause; very gayly*) Are you engaged for this dance?
Amanda Funnily enough I was, but my partner was suddenly taken ill.
Elyot (*rising and going to the radiogram*) It's this damned smallpox epidemic.
Amanda No, as a matter of fact it was kidney trouble.
Elyot You'll dance it with me I hope? (*He starts the music*)
Amanda (*rising and crossing to* L C) I shall be charmed.
Elyot (*as they dance*) Quite a good floor, isn't it? (*They cross below the
    settee to* R C)
Amanda Yes, I think it needs a little Borax.
Elyot I love Borax. (*They move* C *below the settee*)
Amanda (*looking out towards the audience*) Is that the Grand Duchess
    Olga lying under the piano?
Elyot Yes, her husband died a few weeks ago, you know, on his way back
    from Pulborough. So sad.
Amanda (*as they move to* R C) What on earth was he doing in Pulborough?
Elyot (*moving above the table*) Nobody knows exactly, but there have been
    the usual stories.
Amanda I see.
Elyot Delightful parties Lady Bundle always gives, doesn't she?
Amanda Entrancing. Such a dear old lady.
Elyot (*moving to* R *end of the table*) And so gay: did you notice her at
    supper blowing all those shrimps through her ear trumpet?

They go into a long kiss, during which Elyot steers Amanda in front of the settee, R end, sits her down and at the same time ends the kiss. He crosses to the radiogram and turns it off. Amanda is sitting on the edge of the settee, pensively

Elyot (*turning and leaning back against the radiogram*) What are you thinking about?

Amanda Nothing in particular.

Elyot Come on, I know that face.

Amanda Poor Sibyl.

Elyot Sibyl?

Amanda Yes, I suppose she loves you terribly.

Elyot Not as much as all that, she didn't have a chance to get really under way.

Amanda I expect she's dreadfully unhappy.

Elyot (*moving to L of the settee*) Oh, do shut up, Amanda, we've had all that out before.

Amanda (*putting her feet up and settling back into the R-hand corner*) We've certainly been pretty busy trying to justify ourselves.

Elyot (*sitting at the L end of the settee, putting his feet up and nursing Amanda's feet in his R arm*) It isn't a question of justifying ourselves, it's the true values of the situation that are really important. The moment we saw one another again we knew it was no use going on. We knew it instantly really, although we tried to pretend to ourselves that we didn't. What we've got to be thankful for is that we made the break straight away, and not later.

Amanda You think we should have done it anyhow?

Elyot Of course, and things would have been in a worse mess than they are now.

Amanda And what if we'd never happened to meet again. Would you have been quite happy with Sibyl?

Elyot I expect so.

Amanda Oh, Elyot!

Elyot You needn't look so stricken. It would have been the same with you and Victor. Life would have been smooth, and amicable, and quite charming, wouldn't it?

Amanda Poor dear Victor. He certainly did love me.

Elyot (*giving her a quick look*) Splendid.

Amanda When I met him I was so lonely and depressed, I felt that I was getting old, and crumbling away unwanted.

Elyot It certainly is horrid when one begins to crumble.

Amanda looks at him and then away again

Amanda (*wistfully*) He used to look at me hopelessly like a lovely spaniel, and I sort of melted like snow in the sunlight.

Elyot That must have been an edifying spectacle.

Amanda Victor really had a great charm.

Elyot (*putting his feet on the floor*) You must tell me all about it.

Amanda He had a positive mania for looking after me, and protecting me.

Elyot That would have died down in time, dear.

Amanda You mustn't be rude, there's no necessity to be rude.

Elyot I wasn't in the least rude, I merely made a perfectly rational statement.

Amanda Your voice was decidedly bitter.

Elyot Victor had glorious legs, hadn't he? And fascinating ears.

Amanda Don't be silly.

Elyot He probably looked radiant in the morning, all flushed and tumbled on the pillow.

Amanda I never saw him on the pillow.

Elyot I'm surprised to hear it.

Amanda (*sitting up, her feet on the floor; angrily*) Elyot!

Elyot There's no need to be cross.

Amanda What did you mean by that?

Elyot (*rising*) I'm sick of listening to you yap, yap, yap, yap, yap, yapping about Victor.

Amanda (*rising*) Now listen, Elyot, once and for all——

Elyot Oh my dear, Sollocks! Sollocks!—two minutes—Sollocks.

Amanda But——

Elyot (*firmly*) Sollocks!

They both sit on the settee. Elyot looks at his watch. They both look at each other and then away again. Amanda rises and moves up to the piano. She picks up a magazine and stands in the waist of the piano looking at it. Elyot waits a few seconds then rises and moves round the L end of the settee to the table. Amanda comes down to the table. Elyot takes one cigarette from the box on the table; Amanda takes one too. Elyot picks up the matches from the R end of the table with his R hand. With his R arm round Amanda he lights her cigarette; she gives him her cigarette and he puts his in her mouth and she lights it. Amanda crosses to the window; Elyot follows her. They kiss; Elyot puts his L arm round Amanda and they come down to the settee and sit, Elyot R, Amanda L. Elyot looks at his watch

That was a near thing.

Amanda It was my fault. I'm terribly sorry, darling.

Elyot I was very irritating, I know I was. I'm sure Victor was awfully nice, and you're perfectly right to be sweet about him.

Amanda That's downright handsome of you. Sweetheart! (*She kisses him*)

Elyot (*leaning back with her on the settee*) I think I love you more than ever before. Isn't it ridiculous? Put your feet up.

Amanda puts her legs across his, and they snuggle back together in the L corner of the settee, his head resting on her shoulder, and his L arm round her waist

Amanda Comfortable?

Elyot Wait a minute. (*He sits up, reaches over, and takes the ashtray from the table behind the settee, places it in his L hand and lies back again*)

Amanda How long, Oh Lord, how long?

Elyot (*drowsily*) What do you mean, "how long, Oh Lord, how long?"

Amanda This is far too perfect to last.

Elyot You have no faith, that's what's wrong with you.

Amanda Absolutely none.

Elyot Don't you believe in . . . ? (*He points upwards*)

Amanda No, do you?

Elyot (*shaking his head*) No. What about . . . ? (*He points downwards*)

Amanda Oh dear no.

Elyot Don't you believe in anything?

Amanda Oh yes, I believe in being kind to everyone, and giving money to old beggar women, and being as gay as possible.

Elyot What about after we're dead?

Amanda I think a rather gloomy merging into everything, don't you?

Elyot I hope not, I'm a bad merger.

Amanda You won't know a thing about it.

Elyot I hope for a glorious oblivion, like being under gas.

Amanda I always dream the most peculiar things under gas.

Elyot Would you be young always? If you could choose?

Amanda No, I don't think so, not if it meant having awful bull's glands popped into me. (*She puts out her cigarette in the ashtray Elyot is holding*)

Elyot Cows for you, dear. Bulls for me.

Amanda It must be so nasty for the poor animals, being experimented on.

Elyot (*putting out his cigarette in the ashtray which he transfers to his* R *hand*) Not when the experiments are successful. Why, in Vienna I believe you can see whole lines of decrepit old rats carrying on like Tiller Girls. (*He half sits up and puts the ashtray on the table*)

Amanda (*laughing*) Oh, how very, very sweet.

Elyot (*burying his face in her shoulder*) I do love you so.

Amanda Don't blow, dear heart, it gives me the shivers.

Elyot (*trying to kiss her*) Swivel your face round a bit more.

Amanda (*obliging*) That better?

Elyot (*kissing her lingeringly*) Very nice, thank you kindly.

Amanda (*twining her arms round his neck*) Darling, you're so terribly, terribly dear, and sweet, and attractive. (*She pulls his head down to her again and they kiss lovingly*)

Elyot (*softly*) We were raving mad, ever to part, even for an instant.

Amanda Utter imbeciles.

Elyot I realized it almost immediately, didn't you?

Amanda Long before we got our decree.

Elyot My heart broke on that damned trip round the world. I saw such beautiful things, darling. Moonlight shining on old temples, strange barbaric dances in jungle villages, scarlet flamingoes flying over deep, deep blue water. Breathlessly lovely, and completely unexciting because you weren't there to see them with me.

Amanda Take me please, take me at once, let's make up for lost time.

Elyot Next week?

Amanda Tomorrow.

Elyot Done.

Amanda I must see those dear flamingoes.

There is a pause while they kiss

Eight years all told, we've loved each other. Three married and five divorced.

Elyot Angel. Angel. Angel. (*He kisses her passionately on the shoulder and neck*)

Amanda (*struggling slightly*) No, Elyot, stop now, stop——

Elyot Why should I stop? You know you adore being made love to. (*He kisses her again*)

Amanda (*through his kisses; rather flaunting*) It's so soon after dinner.

Elyot stops kissing her and freezes for a second

Elyot (*sitting up at the R end of the settee and pushing her feet violently on to the floor*) You really do say most awful things.

Amanda (*tidying her hair*) I don't see anything particularly awful about that.

Elyot (*rising and moving R*) No sense of glamour, no sense of glamour at all. (*He moves behind the table C*)

Amanda (*pounding the cushions at the R end of the settee*) It's difficult to feel really glamorous with a crick in the neck.

Elyot Why didn't you say you had a crick in your neck?

Amanda (*sweetly*) It's gone now. (*She sits cross-legged at the R end of the settee*)

Elyot How convenient. (*He takes a cigarette from the box*)

Amanda (*holding out her hand*) I want one please.

Elyot (*throwing her one*) Here.

Amanda Match?

Elyot (*impatiently*) Wait a minute, can't you? (*He lights his own*)

Amanda Chivalrous little love.

Elyot (*throwing the matches at her*) Here.

Amanda (*coldly*) Thank you very much indeed.

There is a silence for a moment

Elyot (*crossing to the window*) You really can be more irritating than anyone in the world.

Amanda I fail to see what I've done that's so terribly irritating. (*She puts the matches on the table, over the back of the settee*)

Elyot You have no tact.

Amanda Tact. You have no consideration.

Elyot (*coming down R*) Too soon after dinner indeed.

Amanda Yes, much too soon.

Elyot That sort of remark shows rather a common sort of mind, I'm afraid. (*He walks up stage*)

Amanda (*sitting up*) Oh it does, does it?

Elyot Very unpleasant, makes me shudder. (*He comes down R*)

Amanda Making all this fuss just because your silly vanity is a little upset.

Elyot (*stopping*) Vanity. What do you mean, vanity?

Amanda You can't bear the thought that there are certain moments when our chemical, what d'you call 'ems, don't fuse properly.

Elyot (*derisively*) Chemical what d'you call 'ems? Please try to be more explicit.

Amanda You know perfectly well what I mean, and don't you try to patronize me.

Elyot (*moving to the* R *end of the settee; loudly*) Now look here, Amanda——

Amanda (*rising; suddenly*) Darling, Sollocks! Oh, for God's sake. Sollocks!

Elyot But listen——

Amanda Sollocks, Sollocks! Oh dear—triple Sollocks!

They stand looking at one another in silence for a moment, then Amanda flings herself down on the sofa and buries her face in the cushions. Elyot looks at her, then crosses rapidly to the piano. He stamps out his cigarette in the ashtray, sits and begins to play the Rhapsody in C, by Dohnanyi. At the end he blows a kiss to Amanda who looks at him from the settee. He starts the Étude in A Flat Major, Op. 25, by Chopin. Amanda rises, moves up to the double doors and switches off all the lights except the table lamp up R. *She crosses to the window, puts out her cigarette in the ashtray on the table up* R, *and kneels with one knee on the window seat. Elyot finishes the Chopin and starts "Some Day I'll Find You". Half-way through, Amanda turns and picks up the tune, whistling it. Elyot joins in. Amanda sits on the piano stool,* R *of Elyot with her back to the audience. She plays the last seven notes with one finger, an octave higher than Elyot. With his* L *arm he pulls her across him*

Elyot (*after a moment*) You're the most thrilling, exciting woman that was ever born.

Amanda (*lying in his arms*) Dearest, dearest heart . . .

They hold a long kiss until the telephone bell rings violently. Amanda leaps to her feet and stands down R *of the piano stool*

Elyot (*rising*) Good God!

Amanda Do you think it's them?

Elyot I don't know.

Amanda Nobody knows we're here except Freda, and she wouldn't ring up.

Elyot It must be them then.

Amanda What are we to do?

Elyot (*suddenly turning to Amanda and taking her by the shoulders*) We're all right, darling, aren't we—whatever happens?

Amanda Now and always, sweet.

Elyot (*kissing her*) I don't care, then. (*He crosses to the telephone, switches on the lights at the switch* L *of the double doors and picks up the phone which is still ringing*)

Amanda (*coming down* R *and kneeling on the settee, her back to the audience*) It was bound to come sooner or later.

Elyot (*on the telephone*) Hallo—hallo. . . . What. . . . Comment? . . . Madame, qui? . . . 'Allo—'allo—oui c'est ca. . . . Oh, Madame Duvallon. . . . Oui, oui, oui. (*He puts his hand over the mouthpiece*) It's only somebody wanting to talk to the dear Madame Duvallon.

Amanda Who's she?

Elyot I haven't the faintest idea. (*Into the telephone*) Je regrette beaucoup

Monsieur, mais Madame Duvallon viens de partir—cette apres midi, pour Madagascar. (*He hangs up the telephone*) Whew; that was a close shave. (*He comes down* L *to the tub chair*)

Amanda It sent shivers up my spine.

Elyot What shall we do if they suddenly walk in on us?

Amanda (*sitting on the settee,* R *end*) Behave exquisitely.

Elyot With the most perfect poise?

Amanda Certainly, I shall probably do a court curtsy.

Elyot (*crossing to* L *of the settee*) Things that ought to matter dreadfully, don't matter at all when one's happy, do they?

Amanda What is so horrible is that one can't stay happy.

Elyot Darling, don't say that.

Amanda It's true. The whole business is a very poor joke.

Elyot (*teasing*) Meaning that sacred and beautiful thing, Love?

Amanda (*very serious*) Yes, meaning just that.

Elyot (*facing out front; dramatically*) What does it all mean, that's what I ask myself in my ceaseless quest for ultimate truth. (*He breaks* L) Dear God, what does it all mean?

Amanda Don't laugh at me, I'm serious.

Elyot (*turning to her; seriously*) You mustn't be serious, my dear one, it's just what they want.

Amanda Who's they?

Elyot (*moving in to the settee and leaning on the* L *arm*) All the futile moralists who try to make life unbearable. Laugh at them. Be flippant. Laugh at all their sacred shibboleths. Flippancy brings out the acid in their damned sweetness. (*He sits on the settee,* L *end*)

Amanda (*sitting upright, facing him*) If I laugh at everything, I must laugh at us, too.

Elyot (*sitting upright, facing her*) Certainly you must. We're figures of fun all right.

Amanda How long will it last, this ludicrous, overbearing love of ours?

Elyot Who knows?

Amanda Shall we always want to bicker and fight?

Elyot No, that desire will fade, along with our passion.

Amanda Oh dear, shall we like that?

Elyot It all depends on how well we've played.

Amanda (*seriously*) What happens if one of us dies? Does the one that's left still laugh?

Elyot (*very sophisticated, to cheer her*) Yes, yes, with all his might.

Amanda (*wistfully, clutching his hand*) That's serious enough, isn't it?

Elyot No, no, it isn't. Death's very laughable, such a cunning little mystery. All done with mirrors.

Amanda Darling, I believe you're talking nonsense.

Elyot So is everyone else in the long run. Let's be superficial and pity the poor philosophers. Let's blow trumpets and squeakers, and enjoy the party as much as we can, like very small, quite idiotic, school-children. Let's savour the delight of the moment. Come and kiss me, darling, before your body rots, and worms pop in and out of your eye sockets. (*He pushes her back into the settee and kisses her. Very sweetly*) I don't mind what you do see? You can paint yourself bright green all over, and dance naked in the Place Vendôme, and rush off madly with all the men in the world, and I shan't say a word, as long as you love me best.

Amanda Thank you, dear. The same applies to you, except that if I catch you so much as looking at another woman, I'll kill you.

Elyot Do you remember that awful row we had in Venice?

Amanda Which particular one?

Elyot The one when you bought that little painted wooden snake on the Piazza, and put it on my bed.

Amanda Oh Charles. That was his name, Charles. He did wriggle so beautifully.

Elyot Horrible thing, I hated it.

Amanda Yes, I know you did. You threw it out of the window into the Grand Canal. I don't think I'll ever forgive you for that.

Elyot How long did the row last?

Amanda It went on intermittently for days.

Elyot The worst one was in Cannes when your curling irons burnt a hole in my new dressing-gown. (*He laughs*)

Amanda It burnt my comb, too, and all the towels in the bathroom.

Elyot That was a rouser, wasn't it?

Amanda That was the first time you ever hit me.

Elyot I didn't hit you very hard.

Amanda The manager came in and found us rolling on the floor, biting and scratching like panthers. Oh dear, oh dear... (*She laughs helplessly*)

Elyot I shall never forget his face.

They both collapse with laughter

Amanda How ridiculous, how utterly, utterly ridiculous.

Elyot We were very much younger then.

Amanda And very much sillier.

Elyot As a matter of fact the real cause of that row was Peter Burden.

Amanda sits up slowly

Amanda You knew there was nothing in that.

Elyot I didn't know anything of the sort, you took presents from him.

Amanda Presents: only a trivial little brooch.

Elyot (*sitting up*) I remember it well, bristling with diamonds. In the worst possible taste.

Amanda Not at all, it was very pretty. I still have it, and I wear it often.

Elyot You went out of your way to torture me over Peter Burden.

Amanda No, I didn't, you worked the whole thing up in your jealous imagination.

Elyot You know he was in love with you.

Amanda Just a little perhaps. Nothing serious.

Elyot You let him kiss you. You said you did.

Amanda Well, what of it?

Elyot What of it!

Amanda It gave him a lot of pleasure, and it didn't hurt me.

Elyot What about me?

Amanda If you hadn't been so suspicious and nosy you'd never have known a thing about it.

Elyot That's a nice point of view I must say.

Amanda (*moving to the* R *end of the settee*) Oh dear, I'm bored with this conversation.

Elyot So am I, bored stiff. (*He rises and moves round the* L *of the settee to the table behind*) Want some brandy?

Amanda No thanks.

Elyot I'll have a little, I think.

Amanda I don't see why you want it, you've already had two glasses.

Elyot No particular reason; anyhow, they were very small ones.

Amanda It seems so silly to go on, and on, and on with a thing.

Elyot (*pouring himself out a glassful*) You can hardly call three liqueur glasses in a whole evening going on, and on, and on.

Amanda It's become a habit with you.

Elyot You needn't be so grand, just because you don't happen to want any yourself at the moment.

Amanda Don't be stupid.

Elyot (*irritably*) Really, Amanda . . .! (*He moves to the tub chair*)

Amanda What?

Elyot Nothing. (*He sits in the tub chair*)

Amanda takes the make-up case off the back of the settee and takes out a small comb. She combs her hair

Going out somewhere, dear?

Amanda No, just making myself fascinating for you.

Elyot That reply has broken my heart.

Amanda The woman's job is to allure the man. Watch me a minute, will you? (*She powders her nose*)

Elyot As a matter of fact that's perfectly true.

Amanda Oh, no, it isn't.

Elyot Yes, it is.

Amanda No, it isn't.

Elyot Yes, it is.

Amanda (*snappily*) Oh, be quiet. (*She shuts the case and puts it on the table over the back of the settee*)

Elyot It's a pity you didn't have any more brandy; it might have made you a little less disagreeable.

Amanda It doesn't seem to have worked such wonders with you.

Elyot (*rising and moving above the table*) Snap, snap, snap; like a little adder.

Amanda Adders don't snap, they sting.

Elyot Nonsense, they have a little bag of venom behind their fangs and they snap.

Amanda They sting.

Elyot They snap.

Amanda (*sitting upright with exasperation*) I don't care, do you understand? I don't care. I don't mind if they bark, and roll about like hoops.

Elyot takes some more brandy

Elyot (*after a slight pause*) Did you see much of Peter Burden after our divorce?

Amanda Yes, I did, quite a lot.

Elyot (*coming down* L) I suppose you let him kiss you a good deal more then.

Amanda Mind your own business.

Elyot You must have had a riotous time.

Amanda doesn't answer

No restraint at all—very enjoyable—you never had much anyhow. (*He moves up* L)

Amanda You're quite insufferable; I expect it's because you're drunk.

Elyot (*stopping and turning*) I'm not in the least drunk.

Amanda You always had a weak head.

Elyot (*coming to the* L *end of the settee*) I think I mentioned once before that I have only had three minute liqueur glasses of brandy the whole evening long. A child of two couldn't get drunk on that.

Amanda On the contrary, a child of two could get violently drunk on only one glass of brandy.

Elyot Very interesting. How about a child of four, and a child of six, and a child of nine?

Amanda (*turning her head away*) Don't be stupid.

Elyot (*witheringly*) We might get up a splendid little debate about that, you know. Intemperate Tots.

Amanda Not very funny, dear; you'd better have some more brandy.

Elyot Very good idea, I will. (*He pours out another glass*)

Amanda Ridiculous ass.

Elyot I beg your pardon?

Amanda I said ridiculous ass!

Elyot (*with great dignity*) Thank you very much indeed. (*He drinks the brandy and turns up stage and stands in the waist of the piano looking at a magazine*)

Amanda rises, crosses to the radiogram and changes the record for a particularly noisy one. She returns to the settee and sits

You'd better turn that off, I think. It's very late and it will annoy the people upstairs.

Amanda There aren't any people upstairs. It's a photographer's studio.

Elyot There are people downstairs, I suppose?

Amanda They're away in Tunis.

Elyot This is no time of the year for Tunis. (*He crosses to the radiogram and turns it off, walks back to the piano and continues to look at his magazine*)

Amanda (*icily*) Turn it on again, please.

Elyot I'll do no such thing.

Amanda Very well, if you insist on being boorish and idiotic. (*She rises, crosses to the radiogram and turns it on again even louder than before. She takes a few dance steps to bring her in front of the L end of the settee*)

Elyot turns the pages of his magazine with increasing speed

Elyot (*slamming the magazine down on the piano*) Turn it off. It's driving me mad.

Amanda (*shouting*) You're far too temperamental. Try to control yourself.

Elyot *shouting*) Turn it off!

Amanda I won't.

Elyot rushes down to the up stage side of the radiogram. Amanda crosses below the tub chair to the down stage side of the radiogram. She arrives as Elyot scratches the sound-box across the record. He steps back. Amanda picks up the record and stands with it in her hand, her back to the radiogram

There now, you've ruined the record. (*She scrutinizes it*)

Elyot Good job, too.

Amanda Disagreeable pig.

Elyot (*taking a step to her, suddenly stricken with remorse*) Amanda darling —Sollocks.

Amanda (*furiously*) Sollocks yourself! (*She breaks the record over his head*)

Elyot (*staggering*) You spiteful little beast! (*He slaps her face*)

Amanda screams loudly and hurls herself sobbing with rage into the tub chair

Amanda (*wailing*) Oh, oh, oh——

Elyot (*crossing to R of her and kneeling*) I'm sorry, I didn't mean it— I'm sorry, darling, I swear I didn't mean it.

Amanda Go away, go away, I hate you!

Elyot Amanda—listen—listen——

Amanda (*swinging her R arm and hitting him backhand*) Listen indeed; I'm sick and tired of listening to you, you damned sadistic bully. (*She rises*)

Elyot (*rising and walking up stage; with grandeur*) Thank you. (*He stalks towards the door in stately silence*)

Amanda throws a cushion out of the tub chair. It misses him

(*He laughs falsely*) A pretty display, I must say.

Amanda (*taking two cushions from the settee and hurling them at him; wildly*) Stop laughing like that.

Elyot Very amusing indeed.

Amanda (*losing control*) Stop—stop—stop—— (*She rushes up stage round the L end of the settee throwing another cushion at him. It passes him and hits the lilies on the piano*)

Elyot pushes Amanda and she knocks over the chair L of the table. She makes a rush at Elyot and he knocks over the chair R of the table

I hate you—do you hear? You're conceited, and overbearing, and utterly impossible! (*She rushes towards the double doors*)

Elyot (*meeting Amanda and grasping her by the shoulders; shouting her down*) You're a vile-tempered, loose-living, wicked little beast, and I never want to see you again as long as I live. (*He pushes her*)

Amanda staggers back, knocks over the drinks trolley and sits with a bump on the small settee up L. *There is a pause. She rises*

Amanda (*very quietly*) This is the end, do you understand? The end, finally and forever. (*She starts for the double doors*)

Elyot meets her at the doors and grabs her by the arms

Elyot You're not going like this.
Amanda Oh, yes I am.
Elyot You're not.
Amanda I am; let go of me. (*She pushes him in the chest*)

Elyot staggers backwards down stage. Amanda follows him a few steps

(*Breathlessly*) You're a cruel fiend, and I hate and loathe you. (*She turns and rushes to the double doors and opens them*)

Sibyl and Victor are standing outside the doors

Thank God I've again realized in time what you're really like. Marry you again, never, never, never. . . . I'd rather die in torment——
Elyot (*rushing after Amanda, grabbing her round the waist and pulling her backwards towards the settee*) Shut up; shut up; I wouldn't marry you again if you came crawling to me on your bended knees . . .

They turn and Amanda goes over backwards on to the settee with Elyot on top of her

. . . you're a mean, evil-minded, little vampire—I hope to God I never set eyes on you again as long as I live.

Amanda and Elyot roll on to the floor. Amanda, on top, bangs his head on the floor. He hits her behind

Amanda (*rising and crossing* L; *screaming*) Beast; brute; swine; cad; beast; beast; brute; devil——

Elyot grasps her foot as she passes and she falls. They both rise and stand screaming at each other

Victor and Sibyl enter the room quietly and stand just inside the double doors, staring at Elyot and Amanda in horror. Simultaneously, Elyot dashes to the door down R *and Amanda to the door down* L *as—*

the CURTAIN *falls*

ACT III

The same. About eight-thirty the next morning

The room is in the same chaos as at the end of Act II. In addition the large settee has been moved in front of the door down R, and the small settee has been placed in front of the door down L. All the doors and the window curtains are closed. (See the Ground Plan for other details)

When the CURTAIN *rises the stage is in darkness. Sibyl is asleep on the large settee* R, *Victor is asleep on the small settee* L *with his feet on the tub chair. He has removed his coat and placed it over his body. Louise enters up* C. *She opens one side only of the double doors. She is a frowsy-looking girl and carries a string bag with various bundles of eatables crammed into it, notably a long roll of bread and a lettuce. She crosses towards the window and falls over the cushion by the piano. She leaves her string bag on the floor and rises*

Louise Merde! Qu'est ce que c'est que ça? Les idiots ils ont tout fichu par terre pour que je me casse le nez. (*She goes to the window and opens the curtains*) Espèce d'imbecile. (*She sneezes and turns and sees the room in its chaos*) Regardez-moi ce gachis. Puis, après tout, si ça amuse les patrons de casser le mobilier, moi je m'en fiche, comme de ma première lignette! (*She picks up the chair at* R C *and sets it upright in the waist of the piano. She picks up the cushion and is about to throw it on to the settee when she sees Sibyl*) Oh la, la. (*She shakes Sibyl by the shoulder*)

Sibyl (*waking*) Oh dear.

Louise (*throwing the cushion on to the settee*) Bonjour, madame.

Sibyl (*bewildered*) What?—Oh—bonjour.

Louise Qu'est-ce que vous faites ici, madame?

Sibyl What—what?—Wait a moment, attendez un instant—oh dear . . . (*She sits up*)

Victor (*sleepily*) What? . . . What's happening?

Louise crosses to Victor

  (*As he sees Louise he swings his feet to the ground*) Oh.

Sibyl puts on her shoes

Louise (*firmly*) Bonjour, monsieur.

Victor Er—bonjour—What time is it?

Louise (*rather dully*) Eh, monsieur?

Sibyl Quelle heure est il s'il vous plait?

Louise C'est neuf heures moins dix, madame. (*She picks up the ashtray and puts it on the piano*)

Victor (*rising and moving to* C) What did she say?

Louise comes behind Victor to L C, *picks up the chair and puts it up* L)

Sibyl I think she said nearly ten o'clock.

Louise crosses to her string bag

Victor (*to Louise*) Er—voulez—er—wake—reviellez Monsieur et Madame —er—toute suite?

Louise Non, monsieur. Il m'est absolument defendu de les appeler jusqu'a ce qu'ils sonnent. (*She looks at them and sees they have obviously not understood a word*) Les idiots.

She goes out through the double doors. Victor and Sibyl look at each other helplessly

Sibyl What are we to do?

Victor (*putting on his jacket; with determination*) Wake them ourselves.

Sibyl No, no, wait a minute.

Victor What's the matter?

Sibyl (*feeling in her handbag for her mirror; plaintively*) I couldn't face them yet, really, I couldn't; I feel dreadful.

Victor So do I. (*He moves up to the piano*) It's a lovely morning.

Sibyl Lovely. (*She sees her face in the mirror and bursts into tears*)

Victor (*moving* C) I say, don't cry.

Sibyl I can't help it.

Victor Please don't, please . . . (*He moves to her*)

Sibyl (*putting the mirror away*) It's all so squalid, I wish we hadn't stayed; what's the use?

Victor We've got to see them before we go back to England, we must get things straightened out.

Sibyl Oh dear, oh dear, oh dear, I wish I were dead.

Victor Hush, now—(*he bends over her*)—hush. (*He straightens up*) Remember your promise. We've got to see this through together and get it settled one way or another.

Sibyl (*sniffling*) I'll try to control myself, only I'm so . . . so tired. I haven't slept properly for ages.

Victor (*crossing to the mirror up* L) Neither have I.

Sibyl If we hadn't arrived when we did, they'd have killed one another.

Victor (*turning to her*) They must have been drunk.

Sibyl She hit him.

Victor (*turning away again*) Well—he hit her, too.

Sibyl I'd no idea anyone ever behaved like that; it's so disgusting, so degrading. Elli of all people—oh dear . . . (*She almost breaks down again, but controls herself*)

Victor (*moving* C) What an escape you've had.

Sibyl What an escape we've both had.

Amanda opens her door and looks out. She is wearing travelling clothes and is carrying a small suitcase. She jumps when she sees Sibyl and Victor

Amanda Oh! Good morning.

Victor (*with infinite reproach in his voice*) Oh, Amanda.

Amanda (*indicating the small settee*) Will you please move this, I can't get out.

Victor moves the settee. Amanda advances into the room and goes towards the double doors

Victor (*following her, on her L*) Where are you going?

Amanda Away.

Victor You can't.

Amanda (*stopping*) Why not?

Victor I want to talk to you.

Amanda (*wearily*) What on earth is the use of that?

Victor I must talk to you.

Amanda Well, all I can say is, it's very inconsiderate. (*She plumps the suitcase down R of the door*)

Victor Mandy, I——

Amanda (*crossing to L of Sibyl; gracefully determined to rise above the situation*) I suppose you're Sibyl; how do you do?

Sibyl turns her back on her

Well, if you're going to take up that attitude, I fail to see the point of your coming here at all.

Sibyl I came to see Elyot.

Amanda I've no wish to prevent you, he's in there, probably wallowing in an alcoholic stupor. (*She moves up to the double doors*)

Victor This is all very unpleasant, Amanda.

Amanda I quite agree, that's why I want to go away.

Victor That would be shirking; this must be discussed at length.

Amanda (*taking off her gloves*) Very well, if you insist, but not just now, I don't feel up to it. Has Louise come yet?

Victor If Louise is the maid, she's through there.

Amanda Thank you. You'd probably like some coffee, excuse me a moment.

She goes out through the double doors

Sibyl Well! (*She rises and moves up to R of the chair by the piano*) How dare she?

Victor (*irritably*) How dare she what?

Sibyl Behave so calmly, as though nothing had happened.

Victor I don't see what else she could have done.

Sibyl Insufferable, I call it.

Elyot opens his door and looks out

Elyot (*seeing them*) Oh God!

He shuts the door again quickly

Sibyl Elyot—Elyot—— (*She rushes over to the door and bangs on it*) Elyot—Elyot—Elyot——

Elyot (*inside*) Go away.

Sibyl (*coming in front of the settee, falling on it and banging her feet up and down*) Oh, oh, oh! (*She bursts into tears again*)

Victor (*below the chair by the piano*) Do pull yourself together, for heaven's sake.

Sibyl I can't, I can't—oh, oh, oh——

Amanda enters. She still carries her hat, handbag and gloves; she puts them on the piano

Amanda I've ordered some coffee and rolls, they'll be here soon. (*As she crosses L C*) I must apologize for the room being so untidy.

Sibyl cries loudly. Victor starts to follow Amanda

Amanda hears Sibyl sobbing and stops and looks at her, and then at Victor; then she goes off into her room again, and shuts the door. Victor follows her to the door and stops

Victor It's no use crying like that, it doesn't do any good.

After a moment, during which Sibyl makes renewed efforts to control her tears, Elyot opens the door immediately behind her, pushes the sofa, with her on it, out of the way, and walks towards the front door. He is in travelling clothes, and carrying a small suitcase and a hat

Sibyl (*rushing after him*) Elyot, where are you going?

Elyot Canada.

Sibyl (*catching him by the R arm*) You can't go like this, you can't.

Elyot (*by the double doors*) I see no point in staying.

Victor (*crossing to L of Elyot*) You owe it to Sibyl to stay.

Elyot How do you do, I don't think we've met before.

Sibyl You must stay, you've got to stay.

Elyot Very well, if you insist. (*He plumps his bag down on the floor by the telephone*) I'm afraid the room is in rather a mess. Have you seen the maid Louise?

Victor She's in the kitchen.

Elyot Good. I'll order some coffee. (*He makes a movement towards the double doors*)

Victor (*stopping him*) No, your—er—my—er—Amanda has already ordered it.

Elyot Oh, I'm glad the old girl's up and about.

Victor We've got to get things straightened out, you know.

Elyot (*looking around the room*) Yes, it's pretty awful. We'll get the concierge up from downstairs.

Victor You're being purposely flippant, but it's no good.

Elyot Sorry. (*He lapses into silence*)

Victor (*after a pause*) What's to be done?

Elyot I don't know.

Sibyl (*with spirit*) It's all perfectly horrible. I feel smirched and unclean as though slimy things had been crawling all over me. (*She crosses* L *to the small settee, and sits*)

Elyot (*coming down* C *a few steps*) Maybe they have, that's a very old sofa.

Victor (*coming down* L *of Elyot*) If you don't stop your damned flippancy, I'll knock your head off.

Elyot (*raising his eyebrows*) Has it ever struck you that flippancy might cover a very real embarrassment?

Victor In a situation such as this, it's in extremely bad taste.

Elyot No worse than bluster, and invective. As a matter of fact, as far as I know, this situation is entirely without precedent. We have no prescribed etiquette to fall back upon. I shall continue to be flippant.

Sibyl Oh Elyot, how can you—how can you?

Elyot I'm awfully sorry.

Victor It's easy enough to be sorry.

Elyot On the contrary. I find it exceedingly difficult. I seldom regret anything. This is a very rare and notable exception, a sort of red letter day. We must all make the most of it.

Sibyl I'll never forgive you, never. I wouldn't have believed anyone could be so callous and cruel.

Elyot (*crossing to* R *of Sibyl*) I absolutely see your point, and as I said before, I'm sorry.

Victor ⎱ Now look here, Chase—— (*He crosses to Elyot's* R) ⎰ (*Speaking*
Sibyl ⎰ Elyot—(*she rises*)—it's absolutely impossible—— ⎱ *together*)

Amanda enters. Throughout the following they all follow her with their eyes

Amanda (*crossing to the piano; in social tones*) What! Breakfast not ready yet? Really, these French servants are too slow for words. (*She smiles gaily*) What a glorious morning. (*She goes to the window*) I do love Paris. it's so genuinely gay. Those lovely trees in the Champs-Élysées, and the little roundabouts for the children to play on, and those shiny red taxis, You can see Sacre Cœur quite clearly today, sometimes it's a bit misty, particularly in August, all the heat rising up from the pavements, you know.

Elyot (*dryly*) Yes, dear, we know.

Amanda (*ignoring him*) And it's heavenly being so high up. (*She comes to the upstage end of the settee* R) I found this flat three years ago, quite by merest chance. I happened to be staying at the Plaza Athénée, just down the road——

Elyot (*crossing to* L *of Amanda; enthusiastically*) Such a nice hotel, with the most enchanting courtyard with a fountain that goes plopplopplopplopplopplopplopplopplop——

Victor (*making a slight move towards* C) This is ridiculous, Amanda.

Elyot (*continuing*) Plop plop plop plop plop plop plop plop plop plop——

Amanda (*overriding him*) Now, Victor, I refuse to discuss anything in the least important until after breakfast.

Elyot Plop!

Amanda I couldn't concentrate now, I know I couldn't. (*She comes in front of the settee and tidies the cushions*)

Elyot (*sarcastically*) What manner! What poise! How I envy it. To be able to carry off the most embarrassing situation with such tact, and delicacy, and above all—such subtlety. Go on, Amanda, you're making everything so much easier. We shall all be playing Hunt the Slipper in a minute. (*He makes a slight move to* L *of Amanda*)

Amanda (*turning to Elyot*) Please don't address me, I don't wish to speak to you.

Elyot Splendid.

Amanda And what's more, I never shall again as long as I live.

Elyot I shall endeavour to rise above it.

Amanda I've been brought up to believe that it's beyond the pale, for a man to strike a woman.

Elyot A very poor tradition. Certain women should be struck regularly, like gongs.

Amanda You're an unmitigated cad, and a bully. (*She takes a step towards him*)

Elyot And you're an ill-mannered, bad-tempered slattern.

Amanda (*loudly*) Slattern, indeed!

Elyot Yes, slattern, slattern, slattern, and fishwife.

Victor (*coming to* L *of Elyot and swinging him round*) Keep your mouth shut, you swine!

Elyot Mind your own damned business.

Victor and Elyot start to take their jackets off. Sibyl rushes between them

Sibyl (*a hand on the chest of each*) Stop, stop, it's no use going on like this. Stop, please. (*To Amanda*) Help me, do, do, do, help me——

Amanda I'm not going to interfere. Let them fight if they want to, it will probably clear the air anyhow. (*She crosses to* L C)

Sibyl Yes, but——

Amanda (*crossing back to Sibyl*) Come into my room, perhaps you'd like to wash or something. (*She takes her hand*)

Sibyl No, but——

Amanda (*firmly*) Come along. (*She leads her to* L)

Sibyl Very well. (*She tosses her head at Elyot*)

Amanda drags Sibyl off L

Victor (*taking off his jacket and throwing it on the small settee,* L; *belligerently*) Now then!

Elyot Now then what?

Victor Are you going to take back those things you said to Amanda?

Elyot (*putting his jacket on*) Certainly, I'll take back anything, if only you'll stop bellowing at me.

Victor (*contemptuously*) You're a coward, too.

Elyot They want us to fight, don't you see?

Victor No, I don't. Why should they?

Elyot Primitive feminine instincts—warring males—very enjoyable.

Victor You think you're very clever, don't you? (*He crosses to the small settee and picks up his jacket*)

Elyot I think I'm a bit cleverer than you, but apparently that's not saying much.

Victor (*throwing down his coat again; violently*) What?

Elyot Oh, do sit down. (*He indicates the settee* R)

Victor I will not.

Elyot Well, if you'll excuse me, I will. I'm extremely tired.

Victor (*moving to* C) Oh, for God's sake, behave like a man.

Elyot (*sitting on the settee,* R*; patiently*) Listen a minute, all this belligerency is very right and proper and highly traditional, but if only you'll think for a moment, you'll see that it won't get us very far.

Victor To hell with all that.

Elyot I should like to explain that if you hit me, I shall certainly hit you, probably equally hard, if not harder. I'm just as strong as you, I should imagine. Then you'd hit me again, and I'd hit you again, and we'd go on until one or the other was knocked out. Now, if you'll explain to me satisfactorily how all that can possibly improve the situation, I'll tear off my coat, and we'll go at one another hammer and tongs, immediately.

Victor It would ease my mind.

Elyot Only if you won.

Victor I should win all right.

Elyot Want to try?

Victor Yes.

Elyot (*jumping up*) Here goes then—— (*He tears off his jacket and throws it on the settee,* R)

Victor (*holding his hand up like a policeman*) Just a moment.

Elyot Well?

Victor What did you mean about them wanting us to fight?

Elyot It would be balm to their vanity.

Victor Do you love Amanda?

Elyot Is this a battle or a discussion? If it's the latter I shall put on my coat again, I don't want to catch a chill.

Victor Answer my question, please.

Elyot Have a cigarette?

Victor (*stormily*) Answer my question!

Elyot If you analyse it, it's rather a silly question.

Victor Do you love Amanda?

Elyot (*confidentially*) Not very much this morning; to be perfectly frank. I'd like to wring her neck. Do you love her?

Victor That's beside the point.

Elyot On the contrary, it's the crux of the whole affair. If you do love her still, you can forgive her, and live with her in peace and harmony until you're ninety-eight.

Victor You're apparently even more of a cad than I thought you were.

Elyot (*picking up his jacket*) You are completely in the right over the whole business, don't imagine I'm not perfectly conscious of that.

Victor I'm glad.

Elyot It's all very unfortunate.

Victor (*moving towards his jacket*) Unfortunate: my God!

Elyot It might have been worse. (*Moving up* R, *putting on his jacket*)

Victor I'm glad you think so.

Elyot (*his back to Victor*) I do wish you'd stop about being so glad about everything.

Victor What do you intend to do? (*He moves up to the waist of the piano*) That's what I want to know. What do you intend to do? (*He raps the piano three times*)

Elyot I don't know, I don't care.

Victor I suppose you realize that you've broken that poor little woman's heart?

Elyot Which poor little woman?

Victor Sibyl, of course.

Elyot Oh, come now, not as bad as that. She'll get over it, and forget all about me.

Victor I sincerely hope so . . . for her sake.

Elyot Amanda will forget all about me, too. (*He crosses to* L) Everybody will forget all about me. I might just as well lie down and die in fearful pain and suffering, nobody would care.

Victor Don't talk such rot.

Elyot You must forgive me for taking rather a gloomy view of everything, but the fact is, I suddenly feel slightly depressed.

Victor (*crossing to Elyot*) I intend to divorce Amanda, naming you as co-respondent.

Elyot (*picking up Victor's jacket*) Very well.

Victor And Sibyl will divorce you for Amanda. It would be foolish of either of you to attempt any defence.

Elyot Quite.

Victor And the sooner you marry Amanda again, the better.

Elyot I'm not going to marry Amanda.

Victor What?

Elyot (*holding out Victor's jacket*) She's a vile-tempered, wicked woman.

Victor (*turning his back to Elyot and putting one arm in the jacket*) You should have thought of that before.

Elyot I did think of it before.

Victor (*firmly*) You've got to marry her.

Elyot I'd rather marry a ravening leopard.

Victor (*turning to him angrily and snatching his jacket*) Now look here. I'm sick of all this shilly-shallying. You're getting off a good deal more lightly than you deserve; you can consider yourself damned lucky I didn't shoot you.

Elyot (*with sudden vehemence*) Well, if you had a spark of manliness in you, you would have shot me. You're all fuss and fume, one of these cotton wool Englishmen. I despise you. (*He crosses up* R)

Victor (*through clenched teeth*) You despise me?

Elyot Yes, utterly. You're nothing but a rampaging gas bag!

He goes off into his room and slams the door. Victor, speechless with fury, puts on his jacket and crosses to the settee, R. *Amanda and Sibyl enter*

Amanda (*brightly*) Well, what's happened?

Victor (*sullenly*) Nothing's happened.

Amanda You ought to be ashamed to admit it.

Sibyl Where's Elyot?

Victor In there.

Amanda What's he doing?

Victor (*turning angrily away*) How do I know what he's doing? (*He moves up to the piano and sits on the chair, facing up stage*)

Amanda (*moving* C) If you were half the man I thought you were, he'd be bandaging himself.

Sibyl (*crossing to* R C; *with defiance*) Elyot's just as strong as Victor.

Amanda (*turning*) I should like it proved.

Sibyl There's no need to be so vindictive.

Amanda (*arms folded*) You were abusing Elyot like a pickpocket to me a little while ago, now you are standing up for him.

Sibyl I'm beginning to suspect that he wasn't quite so much to blame as I thought.

Amanda Oh really?

Sibyl You certainly have a very unpleasant temper.

Amanda It's a little difficult to keep up with your rapid changes of front, but you're young and inexperienced, so I forgive you freely.

Sibyl (*heatedly*) Seeing the depths of degradation to which age and experience have brought you, I'm glad I'm as I am!

Amanda (*with great grandeur*) That was exceedingly rude. I think you'd better go away somewhere. (*She waves her hand vaguely, and moves up to the piano. She stands leaning against it,* R *of Victor*)

Sibyl After all, Elyot is my husband.

Amanda Take him with you, by all means.

Sibyl If you're not very careful, I will! (*She goes over to Elyot's door and bangs on it*) Elyot—Elyot——

Elyot (*inside*) What is it?

Sibyl Let me in. Please, please let me in; I want to speak to you!

Amanda Heaven preserve me from nice women!

Sibyl Your own reputation ought to do that.

Amanda (*irritably*) Oh, go to hell!

Elyot opens the door, and Sibyl disappears inside

(*looking at Victor*) Victor.

Victor (*without turning*) What?

Amanda (*sadly*) Nothing. (*She goes behind the settee,* R. *She looks at Victor, feebly pushes at the settee and grunts*)

Victor turns, sees her, rises and comes down to help

Victor Where does it go?

Amanda Over there.

Victor takes the upstage end of the settee and swings it almost parallel with the footlights

Thank you, Victor.

Victor (*crossing down* R) Don't mention it.

Amanda (*after a pause; coming round the* R *end of the settee to the front of it*) What did you say to Elyot?

Victor (*turning*) I told him he was beneath contempt.

Amanda Good. (*She sits* C *on the settee*)

Victor I think you must be mad, Amanda.

Amanda I've often thought that myself.

Victor (*moving up* C) I feel completely lost, completely bewildered.

Amanda I don't blame you. I don't feel any too cosy.

Victor Had you been drinking last night?

Amanda Certainly not!

Victor Had Elyot been drinking?

Amanda Yes—gallons.

Victor (*coming down a step*) Used he to drink before? When you were married to him?

Amanda Yes, terribly. Night after night he'd come home roaring and hic-coughing.

Victor Disgusting!

Amanda Yes, wasn't it?

Victor (*taking another step towards her*) Did he really strike you last night?

Amanda Repeatedly. I'm bruised beyond recognition.

Victor (*suspecting slight exaggeration*) Amanda! (*He is now down* C)

Amanda (*rising and going to him, putting her hand on his arm*) Oh, Victor, I'm most awfully sorry to have given you so much trouble, really I am! I've behaved badly, I know, but something strange happened to me. I can't explain it, there's no excuse, but I am ashamed of having made you unhappy.

Victor I can't understand it at all. I've tried to, but I can't. It all seems to unlike you.

Amanda (*breaking* R) It isn't really unlike me, that's the trouble. I ought never to have married you; I'm a bad lot.

Victor Amanda!

Amanda (*below the settee, facing front*) Don't contradict me. I know I'm a bad lot.

Victor I wasn't going to contradict you.

Amanda Victor!

Victor (*moving away up* C) You appal me—absolutely!

Amanda (*sitting on the* L *end of the settee*) Go on, go on, I deserve it.

Victor (*coming to* L *of the settee*) I didn't come here to accuse you; there's no sense in that!

Amanda What did you come here for, then?

Victor To find out what you want me to do.

Amanda Divorce me, I suppose, as soon as possible. I won't make any difficulties. I'll go away, far away, Morocco, or Tunis, or somewhere. I shall probably catch some dreadful disease, and die out there, all alone—oh dear! (*She sits with her chin cupped in her hands*)

Victor It's no use pitying yourself.

Amanda I seem to be the only one who does. I might just as well enjoy it. (*She sniffs*) I'm thoroughly unprincipled; Sibyl was right!

Victor (*turning away to* c) Sibyl's an ass.

Amanda (*brightening slightly*) Yes, she is rather, isn't she? I can't think why Elyot ever married her.

Victor (*taking a step towards her*) Do you love him?

Amanda She seems so insipid, somehow——

Victor (*taking another step towards her*) Do you love him?

Amanda Of course she's very pretty, I suppose, in rather a shallow way, but still——

Victor Amanda!

Amanda What?

Victor You haven't answered my question.

Amanda I've forgotten what it was.

Victor (*turning away*) You're hopeless—hopeless.

Amanda (*rising and moving to him*) Don't be angry, it's all much too serious to be angry about.

Victor You're talking utter nonsense! (*He turns to her*)

Amanda No, I'm not, I mean it. It's ridiculous for us all to stand round arguing with one another. You'd much better go back to England and let your lawyers deal with the whole thing. (*She moves up to the window*)

Victor But what about you?

Amanda Oh, I shall be all right.

Victor (*moving to* L *of the chair by the piano*) I only want to know one thing, and you won't tell me.

Amanda What is it?

Victor Do you love Chase?

Amanda (*coming to the downstage end of the piano keyboard*) No, I hate him. When I saw him again suddenly at Deauville, it was an odd sort of shock. It swept me away completely. He attracted me; he always has attracted me, but only the worst part of me. I see that now.

Victor I can't understand why. He's so terribly trivial and superficial.

Amanda That sort of attraction can't be explained, it's a sort of chemical what d'you call 'em.

Victor Yes; it must be!

Amanda (*turning to him*) I don't expect you to understand, and I'm not going to try to excuse myself in any way. Elyot was the first love affair of my life, and in spite of all the suffering he caused me before, there must have been a little spark left smouldering, which burst into flame when I came face to face with him again. I completely lost grip of myself and behaved like a fool, for which I shall pay all right, you needn't worry about that. But perhaps one day, when all this is dead and done with, you and I might meet and be friends. That's something to hope for, anyhow. Good-bye, Victor dear. (*She holds out her hand*)

Victor (*shaking her hand mechanically*) Do you want to marry him?

Amanda I'd rather marry a boa constrictor.

Victor I can't go away and leave you with a man who drinks and knocks you about.

Amanda (*coming down to the settee,* R, *and sitting on the* L *arm*) You needn't worry about leaving me, as though I were a sort of parcel. I can look after myself.

Victor (*coming down* L *of the settee*) You said just now you were going away to Tunis, to die.

Amanda I've changed my mind, it's the wrong time of the year for Tunis. I shall go somewhere quite different. I believe Brioni—(*she rises and sits* C *on the settee*)—is very nice in the summer.

Victor Why won't you be serious for just one moment.

Amanda I've told you, it's no use.

Victor If it will make things any easier for you, I won't divorce you.

Amanda (*turning to him*) Victor!

Victor (*sitting on the* L *arm of the settee*) We can live apart until Sibyl has got her decree against Chase, then, some time after that, I'll let you divorce me.

Amanda I see you're determined to make me serious, whether I like it or not.

Victor I married you because I loved you.

Amanda Stop it, Victor! (*She turns away*) Stop it! I won't listen!

Victor I expect I love you still; one doesn't change all in a minute. You never loved me. I see that now, of course, so perhaps everything has turned out for the best really.

Amanda I thought I loved you, honestly I did.

Victor Yes, I know; that's all right. (*He rises and moves* C)

Amanda What an escape you've had.

Victor I've said that to myself often during the last few days.

Amanda There's no need to rub it in.

Victor Do you agree about the divorce business?

Amanda Yes. It's very, very generous of you.

Victor Perhaps Sibyl will change her mind about divorcing Chase.

Amanda Perhaps. She certainly went into the bedroom with a predatory look in her eye.

Victor Would you be pleased if that happened? (*He moves to* L *of the settee*)

Amanda Delighted.

Elyot and Sibyl enter. They come behind the settee; Elyot on the L. *Amanda eases into the* R *corner of the settee*

Sibyl (*looking at Amanda triumphantly*) Elyot and I have come to a decision.

Victor takes a step up stage

Amanda How very nice!

Victor What is it?

Amanda Don't be silly, Victor. Look at their faces.

Elyot Feminine intuition, very difficult.

Amanda (*looking at Sibyl*) Feminine determination, very praiseworthy.

Sibyl I am not going to divorce Elyot for a year. (*She takes his arm*)

Amanda I congratulate you.

Elyot (*defiantly*) Sibyl has behaved like an angel.

Amanda Well, it was certainly her big moment.

Louise appears at the open half of the double doors with a large tray. Unable to get through she bangs the tray against the closed door. Victor moves up stage and opens it for her

Elyot (*crossing to the drinks trolley, indicating the table*) Il faut le mettre sur la table.
Louise Oui, monsieur.

Victor turns to the R end of the table and he and Elyot move it to C. Louise puts the tray down. Amanda and Sibyl eye one another

Amanda It all seems very amicable.

Louise goes up stage between the piano and stool

Sibyl It is, thank you.
Amanda I don't wish to depress you, but Victor isn't going to divorce me, either.

Louise moves the magazines from the stool to the piano

Elyot (*looking up sharply*) What!
Amanda I believe I asked you once before this morning, never to speak to me again.
Elyot I only said "What". It was a general exclamation denoting extreme satisfaction.

Louise picks up the stool, overbalances and sits on the keyboard

Louise Pardon, madame—Ça n'est pas ma faute, mais si madame n'avait pas laissé son piano ouvert, je ne me serai pas cogné dedans. (*She has come down stage and now bangs the stool down above the table*) Pardon,

They all look at Louise

Oh! Puis qu'ils se me haut à table qu'ils boivent leurs café et qu'ils me fichent la paix!

She exits, banging the double doors

Amanda (*moving above the table; politely to Sibyl*) Do sit down, won't you?
Sibyl I'm afraid I must be going now. I'm catching the *Golden Arrow*; it leaves at twelve.

Victor brings the chair by the piano to R of the table

Elyot (*coaxingly*) You have time for a little coffee, surely? (*He brings the chair up L to L of the table*)
Sibyl No, I really must go!
Elyot I shan't be seeing you again for such a long time.
Amanda (*brightly*) Living apart? How wise!
Elyot (*behind his chair; ignoring her*) Please, Sibyl, do stay!
Sibyl (*looking at Amanda with a glint in her eye*) Very well, just for a little. (*She moves to L of the table and sits*)
Amanda (*patting Victor's arm*) Sit down, Victor, darling.

They all sit down in silence; Victor R of the table; Amanda on the C of the stool. Elyot sits on the R end of the stool and pushes Amanda along to the L. Amanda smiles sweetly at Sibyl and holds up the coffee-pot and milk-jug

Half and half?

Sibyl Yes, please.

Amanda (*pouring two cups of coffee; sociably*) What would one do without one's morning coffee? That's what I often ask myself.

Elyot Is it? And what do you always answer?

Amanda Victor, sugar for Sibyl.

Victor passes the sugar

(*To Sibyl*) It would be absurd for me to call you anything but Sibyl, wouldn't it? (*She pours out a third cup*)

Sibyl (*not to be outdone*) Of course, I shall call you Mandy.

Amanda puts down the coffee-pot and looks at Sibyl

Elyot Oh God! We're off again. What weather!

Amanda hands Sibyl her coffee

Sibyl Thank you.

Victor What's the time?

Elyot If the clock's still going after last night, it's a quarter-past ten.

Amanda (*handing Victor a cup of coffee*) Here, Victor dear.

Sibyl lifts her cup

Victor Thanks.

Amanda Sibyl, sugar for Victor.

Sibyl passes the sugar. She stirs her coffee. There is a pause while they all three stir their coffee

Elyot I should like some coffee, please.

Amanda pushes the coffee and milk towards Elyot. He pours some out and bangs down the coffee-pot. They all jump. Sibyl stirs her coffee then starts to drink but is stopped by Amanda's question

Amanda (*to Victor; offering them*) Brioche?

Victor (*jumping*) What?

Amanda Would you like a Brioche?

Victor No, thank you.

There is a slight pause

Elyot I would. And some butter, and some jam. (*He helps himself*)

Sibyl starts to drink again but is again stopped

Amanda (*to Sybil*) Have you ever been to Brioni?

Sibyl No. It's in the Adriatic, isn't it?

Victor The Baltic, I think.

Sibyl I made sure it was in the Adriatic.

Amanda I had an aunt who went there once.

Elyot (*with his mouth full*) I once had an aunt who went to Tasmania.

Amanda looks at him stonily. He winks at her, and she looks away hurriedly. She takes a knife, a plate and a Brioche

Victor Funny how the South of France has become so fashionable in the summer, isn't it? (*He puts down his cup*)
Sibyl Yes, awfully funny.
Elyot I've been laughing about it for months.
Amanda Personally, I think it's a bit too hot, although of course one can lie in the water all day.
Sibyl Yes, the bathing is really divine! (*She puts down her cup*)

They all look at Sibyl

Victor A friend of mine has a house—(*he leans forward*)—right on the edge of Cape Ferrat.
Sibyl Really?
Victor Yes, right on the edge. (*He taps the edge of the table*)

They all peer over the table to look

Amanda That must be marvellous!
Victor Yes, he seems to like it very much. (*He leans back, embarrassed, and crosses his legs*)
Elyot You must tell us about some more of your friends.

The conversation languishes, there is a long pause

Victor ⎱ Now look here——⎱
Sibyl ⎰ I believe——   ⎰ (*Speaking together*)
Amanda (*putting down her cup; with great vivacity*) Do you know, I really think I love travelling more than anything else in the world! It always gives me such a tremendous feeling of adventure. First of all, the excitement of packing, and getting your passport visa'd and everything, then the thrill of actually starting, and trundling along on trains and ships, and then the most thrilling thing of all—(*she picks up her cup*)—arriving at strange places, and seeing strange people, and eating strange foods—— (*She drinks*)
Elyot And making strange noises afterwards.

Amanda chokes violently

Victor (*rising and patting Amanda on the back; to Elyot*) That was a damned fool thing to do.
Elyot How did I know she was going to choke? (*He gives Amanda a resounding smack on the back*)
Victor (*to Amanda*) Here, drink some coffee.
Amanda (*breathlessly gasping*) Leave me alone. I'll be all right in a minute.
Victor (*to Elyot*) You waste too much time trying to be funny.
Sibyl (*up in arms*) It's no use talking to Elyot like that; it wasn't his fault.
Victor (*sitting*) Of course it was his fault entirely, making rotten stupid jokes——

Sibyl I thought what Elyot said was funny.

Victor Well, all I can say is, you must have a very warped sense of humour.

Sibyl That's better than having none at all.

Victor I fail to see what humour there is in incessant trivial flippancy.

Sibyl You couldn't be flippant if you tried until you were blue in the face.

Victor I shouldn't dream of trying.

Amanda and Elyot pick up their cups

Sibyl It must be very sad not to be able to see any fun in anything.

Amanda looks at Elyot. He winks at her again, and she smiles. They hold their cups in mid-air, then put them down again

Victor Fun! I should like you to tell me what fun there is in——

Sibyl I pity you, I really do. I've been pitying you ever since we left for Paris.

Victor I'm sure it's very nice of you, but quite unnecessary.

Sibyl And I pity you more than ever now.

Amanda and Elyot settle down to eating their breakfast

Victor *Why* now particularly?

Sibyl If you don't see why, I'm certainly not going to tell you.

Victor I see no reason for you to try to pick a quarrel with me. I've tried my best to be pleasant to you, and comfort you.

Sibyl You weren't very comforting when I lost my trunk.

Elyot passes jam to Amanda

Victor I have little patience with people who go about losing luggage.

Sibyl I don't go about losing luggage. It's the first time I've lost anything in my life.

Victor I find that hard to believe.

Sibyl Anyhow, if you'd tipped the porter enough, everything would have been all right. Small economies never pay; it's absolutely no use——

Victor (*banging his hand on the table and rising*) Oh, for God's sake, be quiet!

Sibyl (*rising*) How dare you speak to me like that!

Amanda and Elyot lean on the table and watch

Victor Because you've been irritating me for days.

Sibyl (*outraged*) Oh!

Victor You're one of the most completely idiotic women I've ever met.

Sibyl And you're certainly the rudest man I've ever met!

Victor Well then, we're quits, aren't we?

Sibyl (*shrilly*) One thing, you'll get your deserts all right.

Victor What do you mean by that?

Sibyl You know perfectly well what I mean. And it'll serve you right for being weak-minded enough to allow that woman—(*she points to Amanda*)—to get round you so easily.

Victor What about you? Letting that unprincipled roué persuade you to take him back again!

Amanda and Elyot are laughing silently

Sibyl He's nothing of the sort, he's just been victimized, as you were victimized.

Victor (*crossing below the settee to* R) Victimized! What damned nonsense!

Sibyl (*furiously*) It isn't damned nonsense! (*She crosses to Victor*)

Elyot takes Amanda's L *hand in his* R *and kisses it*

You're very fond of swearing and blustering and threatening, but when it comes to the point you're as weak as water. Why, a blind cat could see what you've let yourself in for. When I think of all the things you said about her, it makes me laugh, it does really; to see how completely she's got you again.

Elyot kisses Amanda

Victor You can obviously speak with great authority, having had the intelligence to marry a drunkard.

Sibyl So that's what she's been telling you. I might have known it! I expect she omitted to tell you that she drank fourteen glasses of brandy last night straight off; and that the reason their first marriage was broken up was that she used to come home at all hours of the night, screaming and hiccoughing.

Elyot whispers to Amanda, who nods in agreement

Victor If he told you that, he's a filthy liar.
Sibyl He isn't—he isn't!
Victor And if you believe it, you're a silly, scatter-brained, little fool.
Sibyl (*screaming*) How dare you speak to me like that!

Amanda and Elyot rise quietly and go hand in hand towards the double doors. Elyot puts on his hat and picks up the two suitcases. Amanda picks up her hat and gloves

I've never been so insulted in my life! How dare you!

Victor (*completely giving way*) It's a tremendous relief to me to have an excuse to insult you. I've had to listen to your weeping and wailing for days. You've clacked at me, and snivelled at me until you've nearly driven me insane. I always thought you were stupid from the first, but I must say I never realized that you were a malicious little vixen as well!

Sibyl (*shrieking*) Stop it! Stop it! You insufferable great brute!

She slaps his face hard, and he takes her by the shoulders and shakes her like a rat, as Amanda and Elyot go smilingly out through the double doors, and—

the CURTAIN *falls*

FURNITURE AND PROPERTY PLOT

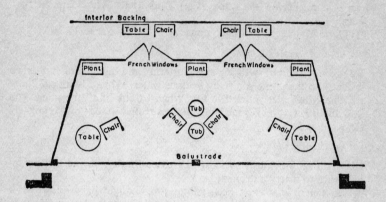

GROUND PLAN

ACT I

On stage: Table, *down* R. *On it:* checked cloth, table lamp, ashtray, silver matchbox

Table, *down* L. *On it:* checked cloth, table lamp, ashtray

4 chairs

Inside R. *window:* table, vase of flowers, chair, picture

Inside L *window:* table, vase of flowers, chair

Up stage R *and* L: Green tub of blue Hydrangea

Up stage C: Green tub of pink Hydrangea

Down stage C: 2 green tubs of Fir trees

On balustrade: R Ivy; L Clematis

Off stage R: Tray with 2 Champagne cocktails

Off stage L: Tray with 2 Champagne cocktails

Personal: **Elyot:** case of cigarettes, lighter.

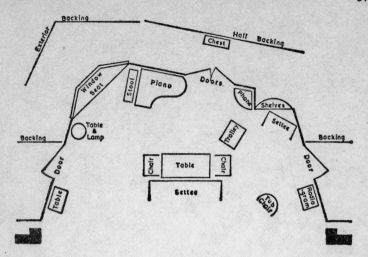

GROUND PLAN

ACT II

On stage: Radiogram. *In it:* record to play, record to break
Mirror
Small settee
Corner cupboard. *On it:* telephone, vase of roses
Piano. *On it:* large glass ashtray, magazines, vase of lilies
On window seat: 3 cushions, magazine
Table, below window. *On it:* lamp, silver ashtray
Table, *down* R. *On it:* vase of roses, silver ashtray, china box. *On shelf:* ornamental cow
Table, C. *On it:* table mats, fruit dish, 2 napkins, 2 fruit plates, knives and forks, 2 brandy glasses, green cigarette box, silver matchbox, 2 mirror ashtrays, cut-glass ashtray, 2 cups of black coffee, spoons, basket of walnuts, nutcrackers
Large settee. *In it:* 7 cushions. *On back:* Shagreen make-up case
Drinks trolley. *On it:* bottle of brandy, other bottles to dress
Tup chair. *In it:* cushion
Shelves, *built in up* L. *On top shelf:* 4 ornaments. *On 2nd shelf:* 4 ornaments. *On bottom shelf:* 2 Cupids, clock
GENERAL NOTE: All Doors closed. Curtains open

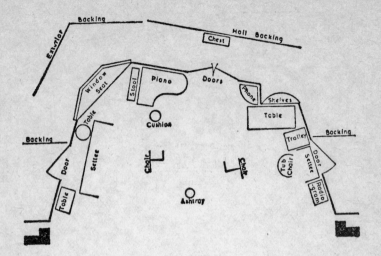

GROUND PLAN

ACT III

On stage:	Large settee across door down R
	Small settee across door down L
	Tub chair in front of small settee
	Table below built-in shelves up L
	Ashtray on floor down C
	Cushion by piano
	2 overturned chairs, RC and LC
	Drinks trolley above small settee
	On piano: empty fruit dish, vase of lilies as they fell
	Under piano: magazines, fruit, cushions
	On stool: 2 magazines
	By radiogram: broken record
Off stage C:	String bag containing lettuce, bread, etc. (Louise)
	Tray with cloth, basket of brioche, coffee-pot, milk jug, sugar basin, butter dish, jampot, spoon, 4 plates, 4 knives, 4 cups and saucers and spoons (Louise)
Off stage R:	Large suit-case, hat (Elyot)
Off stage L:	Small suit-case, hat, bag (Amanda)
	GENERAL NOTE: All Doors and Curtains closed

MUSIC PLOT

ACT I

Cue 1   **Elyot:** "St Moritz. Be quiet."   (Page 4)
                Start, "Land of the Sky-blue Water." (Twice through)

Cue 2   **Elyot:** "Hurry up." (*He saunters down to the balustrade* . . .
                and lights a cigarette)   (Page 10)
                Start, "Some Day I'll Find You."

Cue 3   **Amanda:** "That was no reflection on her, unless she made it
                flatter."   (Page 18)
                Start, "Some Day I'll Find You" (softly)

Cue 4   **Amanda:** (*with dignity*) "Thank you."   (Page 18)
                Increase volume. (Refrain should now be playing)

Cue 5   **Amanda:** "Yes, but Elyot darling——"   (Page 22)
                Elyot: "Solomon Isaacs!"
                Start, "Some Day I'll Find You."

Any character costumes or wigs needed in the performance of this play can be hired from CHARLES H. Fox Ltd, 25 Shelton Street, London WC2H 9HX